Financial Freedom

Financial Freedom (It's Easy When You Know How)

Alexander Fenn

Copyright © 2021 Alexander Fenn

All rights reserved.

ISBN: 9798789020500

To Amelia, thank you for all of your help, support and patience, without which the book would never have been finished.

I promise I'll stop talking about compound interest at the dinner table!

CONTENTS

Preface

1

Introduction

6

What is financial freedom?

16

Earning, spending, owning and owing

26

All you need to know about debt

36

All about pensions

50

A brief introduction to investing

64

Approaches to investing

80

Budgeting techniques

94

The Framework for your financial freedom

102

The financial freedom mindset

106

Framework Step 0 - audit your finances

120

Framework Step 1 - save one month's expenses in an emergency fund

128

Framework Step 2 - maximise your employer pension contributions

138

Framework Step 3 - pay off consumer debt

144

Framework Step 4 - increase your emergency fund

150

The fork in the road: reach for your freedom

156

Framework Step 5 - attack your mortgage

160

Framework Step 6 - invest, invest, invest

168

Ongoing activities for financial freedom

176

Increasing your Wealth Building Fund

184

Side hustles

198

Myths and common questions

204

Concluding thoughts

218

Appendix

222

Preface

Firstly, I would like to say a massive *thank you* for investing your hard earned money in buying this book; I hope you find it as interesting and enlightening as I aimed to make it.

I started writing this book in the middle of the COVID-19 pandemic, during which the instability of our economy and many of our employers became undeniably apparent. What became worryingly clear was that, without the financial support of the government, many of us would be facing financial catastrophes.

The pandemic really opened my eyes to how poorly we manage our money in the UK and inspired me to further research people's finances. What I uncovered was staggering. Did you know, only 22% of people in the UK had no non-mortgage debt going into 2021?[1] Put another way, nearly four in five people had consumer debt! Furthermore, when you delve deeper into these statistics and look at what is being spent on credit cards, almost a third is spent on general living expenses. This is really concerning and suggests that we are living beyond our means and utilising expensive debt to fund the gap.

In addition to typical consumer debt, as a nation we have almost £1.2 trillion of outstanding mortgage debt. This is astounding; we are always told to aspire to buy a house, but I have started to question, at what cost? The nature of debt is that it has a negative financial impact, but I believe the psychological impact is just as pertinent, hugely underestimated and contributing to our deteriorating mental health. This is backed up by the stats, with 44% of people in the UK with debts seeing them as a burden[2] and over 70% of people in the USA experiencing financial stress at least some of the time[3], the effects of which include anxiety, depression, weight gain/loss, relationship difficulties and societal withdrawal.

After the shock caused by the debt level statistics, I thought I would try and find the silver lining to the apparent national personal finance crisis. The UK has an ageing population with more of us living longer, so, surely we at least have enough saved up in retirement savings to provide for a comfortable retirement? The answer, I found, was a resounding, *no*. The average value of a pension pot was just over £63,000 which, although may sound like a lot, is nowhere near enough to provide even a basic lifestyle and is not even 20% of the recommended amount of £237,000 required for a comfortable retirement.[4] Further compounding the issue is that one in five of us in the UK has no form of private or workplace pension.

This lack of personal pension savings means many people in the UK are going to be reliant on the State Pension for their survival during retirement, and it will be, merely, survival. The State Pension age is frequently increasing and someone currently in their 30s could well be in their 70s before they are eligible to claim the State Pension. The state pension is funded by the working population and, as we become an older society, living, and therefore claiming pensions for longer, it seems likely that the value of the state pension will be vastly reduced or even removed. I have come to the realisation that you cannot depend on anyone but yourself when it comes to funding your retirement.

* * *

I have always been an avid saver, a keen investor and had an enterprising spirit (from selling chocolate bars in my high school corridors, to launching a clothing company in sixth form and renting out a flat on Airbnb in my 20s). I have also always sought to improve my personal finances and, in my quest to educate myself to ensure I am doing everything in my power to maximise my financial position, I stumbled across a movement called 'Financial Independence Retire Early' (or 'F.I.R.E'). F.I.R.E has truly changed the way I look at life and has inspired me to spread the word and give people the financial education they never had in school and the tools to take control of their financial future.

My passion is finance. I have two finance degrees and two professional finance qualifications (CIMA and AMCT) and I use the skills and knowledge gained through my profession to coach people on their finances through my business, Alex Fenn Money Mentor. The more I analysed my own personal finance situation in the context of the statistics of the wider population, the more I realised that I have a solid grip on my position and am well placed to assist others with achieving their own financial goals. Whilst I am making great progress towards achieving financial independence, I have sleep walked into numerous financial mistakes, none of which had red flags attached or severe consequences, but which, I realised, are more common than they should be in our society.

The more I thought about it, the more I realised I never had a formal personal finance education; no one ever taught me how to save, how consumer credit or a mortgage actually works or the implications of being in debt. I was only ever told not to take out credit cards and to avoid putting money in the stock markets as they are risky and I might lose that money. I was discouraged from setting up businesses and instead encouraged to go to university, get a *sensible* job to enable me to take out as big a mortgage as I could borrow, and follow the path dictated by society. It dawned on me, though, that whilst this advice was well-intentioned, it was given to me by people who themselves had followed this path and thus wouldn't be retiring until they had spent 45 years working for someone else.

I want to live a different life; I want to live life on my terms and educate others on how they can do so too. I have read every book on personal finance, investing, financial planning and financial freedom that I have been able to get my hands on and, using this knowledge, have pulled together my own Financial Freedom Framework to act as an easy to follow guide to help others achieve their own version of financial freedom.

I intend for this book to provide you with the financial education you likely never received from the formal education system, and provide you with the knowledge and tools needed to understand and proactively manage your personal finances. When you get to the end, I hope that you have the courage and enthusiasm to embark on your financial freedom journey.

It should be noted that, although the core concepts covered by this book are universal, the savings and investment accounts, as well as the tax rates used, are specific to the UK and so may not be relevant to you depending on your location. That said, I am confident you will still find this book incredibly valuable.

Thank you. Enjoy. Good luck!

Introduction

A dream for many of us is to be in a position to not *have* to work for money again. How many times do you find yourself saying to yourself things like: 'if only I won that lottery jackpot'; 'if only I could have bought Google shares ten years ago'; 'if only I could discover a long lost rich relative has left me enough money to pack in the daily grind'? Are you fed up with the commute to a job you don't like, just to pay for your car(s), house(s), holiday(s), clothes? Are you fed up with having to play the office politics game just because you feel you have to in order to be in the running for that next promotion or pay rise? If so, this book will help you re-evaluate your relationship with money and guide you on the way to becoming financially free. Then, you can live life on your terms, whatever that might look like.

People tend to enter the rat race of life and realise too late in the game that they are not fulfilled, having lived their life based on the decisions and opinions of others. Life is there to be lived and enjoyed in whatever way makes you happy, you deserve this and societal norms shouldn't stop you.

From my experience, personal financial education is poor. I personally did not have any financial education during my formal education and the same is the case for many of my friends, colleagues and clients. We are taught from a young age to follow a very specific path in our adult lives:

Step 1) finish school and go to a good University

Step 2) get a steady and secure job with a reputable employer

Step 3) pay into your employer pension

Step 4) get a 25-35 year mortgage and buy the most expensive house you can afford, trading up as and when you can

Step 5) retire with your employer and state pensions and downsize to a smaller house to free up cash to further subsidise your retirement

This is the advice I received throughout my childhood (and I imagine you did too). It is perceived as the safe and secure option from our closest advisors; parents don't want their children to struggle financially and they probably followed the same steps, school reputations are founded on the number of their students that go onto University, Universities attract future students based on how many of their past students go onto work for recognisable brands, employers want consistent and loyal employees, and the bank likes to earn thousands from lending people mortgages.

At no point in school are we taught: what the implications of a mortgage are; about the dangerous cycle of consumer credit; or the potential benefits of investing in the financial markets, living a life below our means or being entrepreneurial. It is unsurprising that, with this lack of financial education, personal debt levels in the UK are at an all time high, with around 70% of people in the UK having less than £1,000 in savings and being only one lost pay day away from being in financial difficulty.[1] Compounding all of this is a lack of retirement savings, meaning someone in their thirties is likely going to have to work well into their seventies. Surely there is a better way to live than under such financial pressure? You may think that the answer to breaking this cycle is, obviously, to 'earn more money', but this isn't necessarily the case. From my experience as a finance coach, it is evident that no matter what someone's salary, their net monthly position doesn't seem to be much different. This begs the question, if the inputs, no matter how big, result in the same output, then what is going wrong in the middle? This middle processor is where financial freedom lies, and this book will explain how to fix it.

How can the inhabitants of such a rich and prosperous country find themselves in such a terrible situation? The lack of financial education combined with a bombardment of sophisticated adverts (it is estimated that we see over four thousand adverts daily)[2] and an abundance of credit (be this be from 'buy now, pay later' (BNPL) services, traditional credit cards or loans); it has never been easier or cheaper to borrow money to buy things. There are almost 63 million credit cards in circulation in the UK and the BNPL market is worth almost £2.7 billion annually and growing[3]. Rewind 50 years and that generation had to save up for everything in order to buy it with cash. The closest thing to credit was paying for something in weekly or monthly instalments and only when the item was fully paid for upfront could you finally have the item. This is the exact opposite of what happens today where you get the item without the need to pay a penny (for now!). Remember the time when you had to save up your hard earned money to buy that new jacket, new phone, or for that meal out, or else you couldn't get it? No, I didn't think so! We are in a society which values owning material possessions immediately and in which deferring our freedom in order to pay for it by trading our time for money with an employer is the norm. This is counterintuitive and is not the route to happiness; how many people on their deathbed wished they could have spent just that bit longer at work to pay for the latest model of smartphone or newest range of designer clothes? In fact, the UK appears 18th in the 2021 'world happiness ranking',[4] so clearly our way of living is not improving our happiness.

That said, there are times where access to credit is hugely helpful and allows people to buy essential items in times of emergency. For instance, if your fridge or oven breaks and you don't have an emergency fund, being able to spread payments over time can be a genuine life saver. Where people get into trouble is when consumer debt just becomes part of the financial furniture and is abused to buy our WANTS, rather than our NEEDS.

It is therefore vital to recognise that our wants are never ending. There is always something new or something different that we don't have, and we are made to feel inferior for not having it. There needs to come a point where you have a balance of having just enough and within this balance lies contentment and happiness. In the later chapters, we will explore the Swedish concept of 'Lagom' which translates to 'not too much, not too little, the right amount', and, applied to every aspect of life, can make a huge difference to the way you view life going forward. The fact that Sweden is the 6th happiest country in the world in 2021 is no coincidence.

It is easy to understand how people get into a bad financial position but becoming financially free can become a reality much easier than you might think. Not only has technology made it easier to borrow money on credit, but it has also never been easier to invest, earn additional income from the 'gig' economy, work remotely, or scale a business. It is these opportunities that you can leverage in your quest for financial freedom.

As grand as it sounds, financial freedom is about understanding some core financial concepts, learning fundamental budgeting techniques, and applying them consistently and with discipline. I am an avid follower of the financial freedom movement having read countless books and blogs and watched hundreds of hours of content, and from this, combined with my professional experience, I have developed my own 'Financial Freedom Framework' which provides a step by step guide to achieving your financial freedom, putting you in a position to live life on your terms.

The aim of this book is to help address the lack of personal financial education and equip you with the tools and attitude you need to be successful with your money. Yes, financial freedom requires you to go against the grain and change your way of thinking from short term instant gratification to long term deferred gratification, set goals and have discipline, but it is there for the taking if you want it and are prepared to put the effort in! Some of your core beliefs will be tested along the way and often the concepts will contradict what you have already been taught but what I can say, with confidence, is that this book will have a transformative effect on not just your wallet but all aspects of your life and may make you realise that financial freedom is much closer than you think. I wish I had read this book before going to University and joining the workforce so I could have taken earlier action and be further along in my personal journey to financial freedom (and avoided some stupid purchases along the way!).

This book is structured in three main parts: firstly, I introduce the concept of financial freedom, then in part two I explain some fundamental finance concepts such as interest, assets, liabilities, investments, and budgeting which are then applied in part three within the context of the 'Financial Freedom Framework'. Worked examples have been provided in the appendix to demonstrate how to put your knowledge in to practice. I don't assume any prior financial knowledge of my readers and the content is intended to be as comprehensive as possible and accessible to all.

The content of this book is for educational purposes only and should not be treated as financial advice.

Key takeaways:
- We are taught from a young age to follow a certain path in life: one which involves taking on debt to educate and house ourselves and trade our time for money over decades, in order to pay for it.
- People's personal finances in the UK are in a bad state, with record debt levels, little savings and the prospect of the young working well into their seventies, something needs to change.
- The lack of formal personal financial education, a proliferation of sophisticated advertising and access to cheap credit make spending money easier than ever before but technology has never made it easier to invest and earn extra money in the 'gig' economy.
- Financial freedom is the conduit between your

current life and your dream life (the one which you live on your terms and makes you happy; the ultimate life goal).
- I have developed my Financial Freedom Framework to provide a step by step guide to help you define and achieve your version of financial freedom, whatever that may be.

*Part One:
Financial
Freedom*

What is financial freedom?

You may have heard of financial freedom, or the concept of it, from one its many pseudonyms. The seemingly most well-known is 'Financial Independence' (from the 'Financial Independence Retire Early' or 'F.I.R.E' movement which has generated a huge following in the USA leading to the emergence of numerous F.I.R.E celebrities such as 'Mr Money Moustache', 'Grant Sabatier', 'The Mad Fientist' and 'Vicki Robin', to name but a few). Within the F.I.R.E movement are a number of sub-categories: lean-F.I.R.E, fat F.I.R.E, and coasting F.I.R.E. Ultimately, they all have the same principle at their core:

'Generating sufficient passive income from your assets, so you no longer need to rely on trading your time for money.'

As a general rule, to be financially free, you need to have 25 times your annual living expenses saved in investments, which will then allow you to withdraw 4% of this per year (known as the safe withdrawal rate) as income to cover your expenses. For example, if you expect to spend £25,000 per year, you will need £625,000 invested in order to be financially free. The 4% rule was derived from something called the 'Trinity Study', which evaluated how long someone's retirement portfolio would last under various draw down rates and asset allocations (being the percentage split between equities and bonds) from 1925 to 1995.

Critics of the 4% rule suggest that the low interest rate we currently live with makes it harder to earn sufficient returns over and above inflation, making the 4% withdrawal rate too aggressive. The 4% rule has been successful historically and I still use it as an assumption in my own financial planning as well as for my clients but if, after evaluating the literature, you believe this to be too risky, you can always use a 3% assumption which will give you more than enough headroom; you then simply need 33 (rather than 25) times your annual living expenses saved in investments and use a 3% withdrawal rate.

Financial freedom, having the ability to do what you want, when you want, does not mean that you have to stop working, after all, work is good for the soul and, often, gives someone a sense of purpose. Many people who become financially free continue working in one way or another, but the difference is that they only do it if they WANT to, not because they HAVE to - this choice is what financial freedom is all about and why it is so appealing. Of course, you can continue with your current job if it makes you happy but this is unlikely to be the case given that, in the UK, more than three quarters of people are unhappy in their jobs with a fifth of employees in 2020 admitting that their work negatively impacts their health and two thirds stating that they take work stress home.[1] Overall, it can be said, jobs don't seem to be the source of happiness and so the faster we don't have to rely on them, the better.

Before diving into the details of each stage of financial

freedom, you should know that how fast you achieve your freedom is dependent on three main factors: your expenses, your savings rate, and the return on your investments.

- *Expenses:* the more you want to spend, the more money you need invested and the longer it will take to buy your freedom. Someone who needs to cover £25,000 in annual expenses will be in a position to retire earlier than someone who needs to cover £50,000.
- *Savings rate:* the more money you can save each month as a percentage of your income, the faster you will reach your required investment level and the faster you can achieve financial freedom. There is a great early retirement calculator[2] which indicates that someone saving 66% of their income could retire in just over 10 years vs someone saving 16% (France's average) who could retire in just over 41 years or saving 6% (USA's average) who could retire in 62 years (if ever). Your savings rate is so powerful and the main difference between your current existence and financial freedom.
- *Return on investment:* if you are not investing your money in inflation beating assets (equities/bonds/commodities/property) you are not going to benefit from compound interest and will not have enough money to retire early. By way of example, if you invested £10,000 per year for 10 years and earned a 6% return, you would have just under £132,000 compared to if you only earned a 2% return which would yield around £109,000. You need to be earning a good return on your investments, in addition to minimising your expenses and maximising your savings rate, to give you the best chance of achieving

invested, which, given the power of compound interest, will grow to provide enough income for your desired retirement at a more traditional retirement age. As the money is not available yet, but will be later, you can take a job which simply supports your current lifestyle until you can access your retirement savings. For example, you could work part time, change to a less stressful job or a job which better aligns to your moral values. As long as you earn enough to cover your living expenses, you can 'coast' to your retirement.

Stage 6: Financial Abundance

This stage simply means you have so much money you can do whatever you want, when you want, no matter the cost. Someone with a net worth of £25m has financial abundance! The role of someone at this stage is more about preserving their wealth and donating to the greater good of society than the maintenance of their personal lifestyle. The term from the F.I.R.E movement for this is known as *'Fat F.I.R.E'* and it means having so much invested that your 4% withdrawal rate can cover whatever lifestyle you want. This is not really achievable through saving and investing your income from a 9-to-5 job but from owning businesses or demonstrating a very lucrative skillset such as being a professional sportsperson or musician which allows you to save an extraordinary amount of money. For example, drawing down £500,000 per year in passive income from an investment portfolio worth £12.5m!

As you can see, there are a number of iterations of financial freedom and it is up to you what your 'number' is; there is no right or wrong answer, ultimately it is whatever will make you happiest. If you would be happy with a lifestyle that costs you £20,000 per year, no need to wait until you have a portfolio to support £100,000 in passive income. It is crucial to evaluate your life to understand what truly makes you happy and to define what is *your* enough and then remember that for every £1 you spend, you need at least £25 invested to cover this cost. If you really can't live without your gourmet meal box subscription which costs £600 annually, be aware that you need to have £15,000 invested in order to passively fund it (applying the 4% rule).

No matter to what level of financial freedom you aspire, the underlying theme remains the same: save and invest heavily to enable yourself to rely on yourself to live rather than anyone else. The decision as to your desired level of financial freedom is completely yours, it may even be that you are happier earning a smaller income now, than sacrificing more of your time to earn a higher income later. Ultimately, it is about being free to follow your passions and the activities that make you truly happy, without having the pressure to meet financial obligations.

Having now read about the various levels of financial freedom, the different factors pivotal to buying your freedom, and the relationship between the different investment and withdrawal rates, you may be feeling a bit overwhelmed and daunted by the journey ahead, but I assure you that, with some focused effort, mindful decisions, consistency and discipline, achieving your freedom is much easier than it may currently appear.

Key takeaways:

- Financial freedom is all about generating sufficient passive income from your investments to cover your living expenses without the need for you to trade your time for money or rely on an employer for

Earning, spending, owning and owing

Before we dive into the detail of the Financial Freedom Framework and planning your route out of the rat race, it is important to understand some fundamental concepts within finance which will become the cornerstone of your knowledge. This chapter will cover what you earn and spend, what you own and what you owe, as well as the principles of interest and inflation. It is important to understand how all of these elements interact with each other, as being able to control each element will significantly impact your ability to build wealth and buy your freedom.

Assets:

Let's start with the accounting definition of an asset, which is, 'a resource controlled by an entity as a result of past events and from which future economic benefits are expected to flow to the entity'. This sounds a bit complex but, when adapted in respect of personal finance, boils down to:

'A resource we OWN that will increase our future wealth as a result of it increasing in value and/or paying an income from interest, dividends, royalties or rent'. In other words, *'assets generate cash and build wealth'*.

* * *

***

Liabilities:

Simply put, a liability is any amount that you OWE and you will need to use your cash or other assets in order to settle such liability. Some common examples of liabilities include your mortgage, rent, car payments, loans, committed phone contracts and credit cards. One problem with liabilities is that they prevent us from using our income to buy assets, thereby reducing our wealth. Liabilities have never been so easy to acquire as they are today. The prevalence of Buy Now Pay Later offers, instant approval credit cards and pay day loans means we can easily access (borrowed) cash to instantly buy the things we want, without the need to save up beforehand. Our lives are therefore full of 'stuff' bought with borrowed money, all of which becomes one giant liability. It is vital to shift your mindset to start looking at purchases as assets and liabilities. So, the next time you get a pay rise and are tempted to upgrade your lease car for an additional £100 per month, remember that what you are actually signing up to is a long term liability, which, at the end of the term, leaves you with nothing.

Net worth:

Your net worth is the result of adding up all of your assets and deducting your liabilities. If this number is positive, you are in a net asset position (congratulations!); if it is negative, you are in a net liability position. Learning how to calculate, and tracking, your net worth in detail is a vital exercise to be undertaken regularly throughout your journey towards financial freedom, to ensure your net worth is moving in the right direction.

Income:

This is commonly understood and is the money you

receive from either: trading your time for money in the form of a salary or wage from an employer; selling items or assets for a profit; or receiving interest, rent, dividends, royalties, advertising income, sponsorship or something else.

There are two means of generating income: actively and passively. Active income is where there is a direct relationship between your time and your income. Traditionally, this is in the form of a wage from an employer, whereby if you don't turn up, you don't get paid and, as your time is limited to 24 hours per day, your income is limited. Passive income, on the other hand, is not linked to your time and means you can detach the relationship between your time and your income. For example, if you own shares in FTSE 100 companies, they pay you a dividend just for owning it, you don't have to clock in and answer to a boss in exchange for this income.

A key element in achieving your financial freedom is to (i) buy assets that generate you a passive income, and (ii) build assets (such as a business) which can generate an income without the need for you to actively work for it. Passive income is unlimited and, consequently, generating it should become a focus in your quest for financial freedom.

Expenses:
These are your day to day costs of living and include utilities, council tax, petrol, insurance, food, entertainment, internet, phone, holidays, childcare, clothing, transport...you get the idea - there are a lot! It is important to track your expenses thoroughly, so you really understand where you are spending your money and are able to evaluate the value these add to your life. Any expense that is not adding value to your life, get rid of it and redirect the money to buying appreciating assets instead.

* * *

There is a concept with expenses that is a silent killer of people's dreams of retiring early and that is *'lifestyle creep'*. 'Lifestyle creep' means that as your income increases over time, your expenses increase in line with it, such that you never have the excess income left for saving and building assets. For example, you graduate university and earn £30,000 per year and spend £25,000 per year. After 10 years, you earn £50,000 and spend £45,000 because someone with your income becomes more accustomed to eating out, buying designer clothes and driving a nicer car. In each situation, the net amount left for saving is the same, despite a 66% increase in income. I see lifestyle creep all the time when I am coaching clients and the same complaints of, 'not having enough money, savings, investments, pension etc…' always appear, no matter what their income level. When I review expenses in detail, the effects of lifestyle creep are plain to see: costs of the basics are extortionate, there are various subscriptions, higher car costs, higher mortgage costs… simply higher everything. Breaking this cycle is hard but vital in your pursuit of leaving the rat race behind for good.

Your level of expenses also determines how much you need for financial freedom, as well as how quickly you can get there. If your lifestyle creep means your expenses increase each year, it means you need to set aside more and more money to finally quit the rat race. Lifestyle creep equals a longer 'prison sentence'.

Net income or, as I like to call it, your 'Wealth Building Fund' (WBF):

Any income remaining after you have paid out your living expenses and repaid committed liabilities, is your net income or Wealth Building Fund ('WBF'). This should be the 'number' at the forefront of your mind which you should continually aim to increase wherever possible. The idea is to use your WBF to purchase appreciating assets or further reduce your existing liabilities, not to whittle it away on excess purchases. My Financial Freedom Framework that I will introduce you to later, is reliant on you generating the largest WBF possible which you direct towards wealth building activities, ultimately increasing your net worth and taking a step closer towards financial freedom. There are three simple ways to improve your WBF position: increase your income; reduce expenses; or, the best option, do both!

Interest:

It has been said that, 'compound interest is the eighth wonder of the world. (S)he who understands it, earns it… (s)he who doesn't, pays it'. I like this quote from Albert Einstein, as it sums up perfectly the power and importance of understanding interest. The first thing to bear in mind is that there are two categories of interest, *earned* and *paid*.

Earned interest is the compensation you receive for sacrificing the use of your capital today, for its return in the future. The longer you sacrifice your money, the higher the interest rate you should earn; the riskier the investment, the more you should be rewarded as compensation for taking that risk. Conversely, paid interest is the penalty you pay for using someone else's capital in the absence of your own. The longer you use their money, the more interest you pay. Paying interest can be deadly for your financial freedom and too much of this can mean that financial freedom doesn't ever become a reality for you.

The second thing to remember is that there are two types of interest which make a huge difference to how much interest you earn or pay; that is, *simple* vs *compound* interest. Simple interest means you earn interest on the principal balance only, whereas compound interest means the interest earned on the principal balance also earns interest.

Let's look at an example: you put £10,000 into a simple interest savings account paying you 5% per year.

Simple Interest:
- Year 1: £10,000 x 5% = £500 interest earned
- After 5 years: £500 x 5 = £2,500 total interest earned.

Compound Interest:
- Year 1: £10,000 x 5% = £500 interest earned. This earned interest added then to £10,000 gives a new principal of £10,500
- Year 2: £10,500 x5% = £525 interest earned. This earned interest added to £10,500 gives a new principal of £11,025
- Year 3 = £11,025 x 5% = £551 interest earned (new principal is £11,576)
- Year 4: £11,576 x 5% = £579 interest earned (new principal 12,155)
- Year 5: £12,155 x5% = £608 interest earned.

At the end of year 5 you would have earned total compound interest of £2,763 as opposed to £2,500 from simple interest. This may not sound like a lot but time is the friend of compound interest; if we were to use the same investment as above but extrapolate to 20 years, you would earn £10,000 in simple interest over the term, vs £26,533 in compound interest, a massive difference of £16,533! Hopefully now you can see why Einstein was so enthusiastic about the magic of compound interest!

***

Inflation:

Inflation is the general rise in prices in an economy over time. It is really important to understand inflation and factor it into your financial freedom calculations as its impact means the purchasing power of your money reduces over time. Inflation is measured in the UK by the Office for National Statistics by tracking the cost of a basket of goods and services over time, culminating in the 'Consumer Price Index' or 'CPI' for short. The Bank of England has a target of maintaining inflation at 2% per year. In practical terms, inflation means that £100 today is worth less in a year's time (and worth even less in five or ten years). For instance, if inflation were 2% per year, £100 in 5 years would only have the same purchasing power as £78.35 today. This means that if your money is not earning a return equal to or higher than inflation, you are, in effect, losing money.

Key takeaways:
- Assets either appreciate or depreciate. It is important that you are aware of the difference and focus on (i) buying appreciating assets, and (ii) limiting the impact of depreciating assets on your wealth.
- Clear your liabilities and avoid falling into the trap of taking on additional liabilities for the purposes of making unnecessary purchases.
- Income can be earned both actively (by trading your time for money) and passively (whereby the income you earn is not directly reliant on you trading your time e.g. dividends from owning shares).
- Track your expenses and don't fall into the consumerist trap of lifestyle creep where your expenses continue to grow in line with your income.

- Your income less your expenses is known as your Wealth Building Fund and is something you should continually focus on increasing.
- You grow your wealth by maximising your Wealth Building Fund and using it to buy income generating assets.
- Compound interest is simply amazing and means the interest your money earns, also earns interest; it has the power to grow exponentially when compared to earning simple interest.
- Inflation is the general increase in prices throughout an economy and is measured in the UK by the Consumer Price Index with a target of 2% annually, if your money is not earning at least the rate of inflation, you are losing money.

All you need to know about debt

Debt is one of the most important elements of personal finance and will probably be the main determinant of your financial success, so it is vital you understand how it works and what can happen if you are not disciplined and don't stay on top of it. From my time mentoring clients with their finances, it always surprises me how much consumer debt they have no matter what their income. Whilst someone with a higher income may have a lot of nice things to show for it, financially they are no better off than someone with a lower income.

There are many forms of debt, some of which are not actually seen as debt in our society! You need to know that the best way to buy something is with cash and you should only take out debt if you absolutely have to; see it as a last resort, not the first option. You should only use debt to buy items which hold or appreciate in value, borrowing money to purchase basic expenses and consumer goods is a slippery slope and should be avoided. Numerous studies cite the link between problem debt and mental health issues and thus debt should be considered carefully before touching it; liken debt to a house being on fire in front of you requiring you to do whatever you can, as quickly as you can, to put it out.

***

This chapter explains the various types of debt you will encounter and provides some hints and tips on how to best use (or not use as the case may be) each debt.

Interpreting the cost of debt:

The cost of debt, whether a credit card, mortgage or personal loan, is quoted as an interest rate which is a percentage of the principal you borrow. For example, if you borrow £10,000 and repay £11,000, the interest rate is 10%. If you need to borrow money, you should compare deals in order to secure the lowest interest rate (and thus cheapest debt) possible. As money can be borrowed for a period of less than or more than a year, comparing interest rates can be tricky. Each lender will show you an Annual Equivalent Rate ('AER') and it is this rate which shows you how much it would cost you to borrow the money over a one year period and should be used to compare rates and choose the best one. Think of it as comparing the cost per 100g when you are choosing between a large and small jar of coffee in the supermarket. Compound interest also comes into play when taking out debt, but rather than earning it, you will be paying it. The interest on your debt, starts to accumulate so if you don't pay off your debt, your debts can quickly get out of hand.

Consumer debt:

Consumer debt comes in many forms including, credit cards, store cards and 'Buy Now Pay Later' offers, and is the debt you likely receive countless emails and junk mail about containing tempting offers such as:

- 'interest free on purchases for three months', meaning anything you purchase during the three month period from activating your account will be

interest free but anything purchased thereafter attracts the standard rate (usually well over 10% per year); and
- '0% interest on balance transfers for X months', meaning you can transfer a balance from an existing credit card to a new credit card and there will be no interest charged on such balance for the duration of the offer (although there is usually a 1-5% fee for doing this).

Credit cards:

Fifty years ago, in order to look well off, you had to be well off, because people could only buy the status symbols associated with success (think Rolex watches, Chanel handbags, Mercedes-Benz cars) for cash. Things have changed, American Express, MasterCard and Visa will happily lend you thousands of pounds (at around 20% annual interest, I hasten to add), which allows you to buy those status symbols now instead of having to wait and save the cash like the old days. So now you can look rich, without having to be, and the price you pay is your time, which you have to keep trading for money until the credit cards are paid off. To compound the issue, the more someone earns, the more credit is available to them and it is very tempting to see this as a 'reward' for being more successful and, as a result, spend more on treating yourself because now you are earning a certain income. Don't fall into the lifestyle creep trap and risk postponing your financial freedom indefinitely.

Knowing how credit card repayment works is vital in avoiding falling victim to the credit card interest trap. The main problem with credit cards and a common cause of people's problems is that each month you can spend up to your maximum credit limit but, when you login to your account each month to pay, you are prominently given the option to make a 'minimum payment' only (normally between 1% and 3% of the total balance). This 'minimum' amount is exactly what the credit card companies want you to pay and it can be quite tempting to do just that. If your minimum payment is 2% on a £1,000 outstanding credit card balance, your minimum payment could be just £20! So, for £1,000 worth of purchases, you only need to pay £20 - sounds great right? But the fact you haven't cleared your balance means that interest starts being charged from the date of the purchase (not the end of the billing cycle) and this is where the debt trap begins.

To demonstrate how insanely expensive credit cards can be using the above example: if you started with a £1,000 balance, never spent another penny on the card but only paid the minimum payment each month - it would take you 18 years and 7 months to clear it and your total repayments would be £2,336!!

So, if you take anything from this, don't be tempted to just clear the minimum amount in favour of holding onto your hard earned cash; pay off the credit card in full each month and never buy things you can't afford! The reason consumer debt is especially dangerous is that it plays on our emotions and societal pressure to always want more and wanting it now, especially items which show off our social status. Of course, there may be times when an unforeseen event occurs resulting in unforeseen, often unavoidable, spend, for example, your boiler breaks or your roof starts leaking. As mentioned earlier, a credit card can be immensely helpful in this scenario, where the amount needed to cover such cost exceeds the amount available to you in your emergency fund (more on this later). This is where those tempting offers we looked at earlier in this chapter can be used to your advantage. For example, a balance transfer can be a helpful way of clearing sizeable and/or unexpected debts if you are becoming overwhelmed and need to get out of the interest spiral. The word of caution is not to *'avoid these tempting offers at all costs'* but to *'understand how these offers can work for you to clear rather than increase your liabilities'*. Use credit wisely to improve your credit score and clear your debts once and for all, not to run up further credit card debt on useless purchases.

There is also an argument to use credit cards in a positive way to earn rewards, such as air miles or supermarket points, and this system can work but only if you are incredibly disciplined and by this I mean:
- only buy things you would otherwise buy with cash i.e. don't spend more than you normally would just because you have the credit card limit which allows it
- pay off the balance in full every month to ensure you never pay interest
- only take out a reward credit card if you would otherwise buy the things those points can be traded for. For example, if you frequently travel long haul with a certain airline, having a credit card that gives you air miles could be a good idea

I cannot emphasise enough just how careful you have to be with consumer credit. In an ideal world, you would never use it but, in reality, most of us will use it throughout our lifetime. So, if you do, use it wisely and please please please just pay it off in full to avoid any interest payments.

Personal loans:
What if you *want* to purchase an expensive item and don't

have the cash? The answer is simple: resist the temptation. What if you *need* to purchase an expensive item and don't have the cash? You may have the option to borrow the money, usually from a bank. Personal loan terms vary anywhere from between 1 to 5 years and interest rates are generally cheaper than they are on credit cards. There may also be a need to secure the loan either on the item you are buying (e.g. a car) or another of your assets which can be sold by the lender to recover their loan if you fall behind on your payments. Loans, like credit cards, have to be repaid each month but, unlike credit cards, the monthly repayment amount is typically fixed. If you fail to repay your loan, you can be taken to court, your assets may be repossessed and your credit score will be significantly reduced meaning you may not be able to borrow again, or, if you can, interest rates will be extortionate. There are no excuses for missing a payment; lenders don't care about a change in your circumstances and will want their money back.

Using debt to buy a car:

Cars can be a real conflict for people when it comes to finances and outward perception: cars are one of the most visible signs to others of our economic status, so it is tempting to spend as much as possible on your car to show to others just how successful you are! However, cars are one of the fastest depreciating (and let's not forget, expensive) assets you will ever buy, thereby making a huge impact on your financial situation. I have to stress that the car you drive does not correlate to your net worth (see my blog 'revenue for vanity, profit for sanity' for my professional opinion on this).

There are some common options when it comes to using debt to buy a car:
- *Hire Purchase*: this involves putting down an initial

deposit (anywhere from 5% to 20% is normal), followed by monthly repayments for several years (3 to 5 is standard) until you have paid off the car. If you miss your payments, the lender can repossess your car.
- *Personal Contract Purchase*: this involves paying an initial deposit, followed by fixed monthly payments (which will be lower than hire purchase), and then, at the end of the term, the option to either hand the car back, buy the car for the price pre-agreed at the beginning of the contract, or put the value towards the cost of a new car.

It should be noted that with each of these options there can be certain mileage and condition restrictions which could result in you having to pay hefty penalty fees if they are not complied with.

Mortgages:

Growing up in the UK, you will likely have been taught that owning your house is a major financial goal and home ownership is often seen as the pinnacle of success. It is undeniable that owning your house is admirable and aspirational, but, what is often overlooked is that, owning a home and having a mortgage on a house are two very different things but these terms are used interchangeably. To fully understand your financial situation, you need to be aware of the distinction. To be absolutely clear, if you have a mortgage on your house, you do not *own* it; the amount of the house you really own is the house value less any outstanding mortgage. For example, if your house is worth £250,000 and your outstanding mortgage is £200,000, you own (or have equity) worth £50,000 - you *do not* own a house worth £250,000!

* * *

Certainly in the UK, a mortgage is not considered 'real' debt because it underpins an asset that generally appreciates over time. Whilst this is true, a mortgage is still very much a personal debt which needs repaying each month. I am not against mortgages, after all, most people don't have enough cash to buy a house outright. What I am against is the assumption that there is no need to treat a mortgage as real debt and the common view that a mortgage is just something you pay off over 25-35 years because 'that's just what everybody does'. It is really important to understand what a mortgage entails so you know what you are getting yourself into and can make the right decisions for you, both at the outset and for the duration of the mortgage term.

A mortgage interest rate is either (i) fixed (i.e. the interest rate doesn't change), or (ii) variable (i.e. the interest rate changes in line with the Bank of England's base interest rate), for a period of, typically, between 2 and 5 years, following which the rate reverts to the lender's 'Standard Variable Rate' ('SVR') which normally sees an increase to the offer rate of at least 2%. At the point your offer rate expires, you have the ability to, and should, remortgage, allowing you to benefit from a new interest rate lower than the SVR. You should do this at every opportunity throughout the mortgage term. This is also a good time to evaluate whether you are able to reduce the term of your mortgage.

If you put down a £50,000 deposit on a £250,000 house and pay for the rest with a mortgage of £200,000 borrowed over 25 years at an interest rate of 4%, the total amount you will repay is actually £316,570. That's £116,570 of interest (about the cost of a brand new Porsche 911) on top of the principal. It is important to bear in mind that, when you add all this together, your £250,000 house will actually cost you £50,000 + £316,570 = £366,570 (not to mention the added cost of moving which, on average, is over £10,000)![1]

In addition to costing you more than you think, there is another impact of taking out a mortgage and that is, come hell or high water, you need to make your monthly payment. So, fall ill and can't work? Bad luck, you still have to pay your mortgage. Your partner with whom you share the mortgage loses their job? Tough luck, you still have to pay your mortgage. Hate your job and can't find another? You still have to pay your mortgage. The bottom line: if you fail to pay, the bank will take ownership of your house, kick you out, and sell it to get their money back.

Because of the non-negotiable nature of mortgages, I strongly advise you not to maximise the amount you borrow, to allow yourself sufficient headroom each month to absorb any additional costs (e.g. increased energy bills or unexpected essential expenses). You don't want to be in such a precarious situation that a 0.5% increase in the interest rate will make you default on your payments. On this basis, I would suggest your mortgage payment is an absolute maximum of 30% of your take home pay (although, ideally this would be lower).

Mortgages, although a necessity for most of us, can be lethal to your financial situation if you are not careful. A mortgage is real debt and can really tie you down and limit your prospects, given that you have to pay it no matter what happens. This is why it is vital to be aware of what a mortgage is and sign up to one, only with your eyes open; see it as something to clear as soon as you can, rather than something to be taken out as a sign of your success.

* * *

Assuming very few of us are in the ideal position of being able to buy a house for cash, stick to these key rules if you need to take out a mortgage to get onto the property ladder:
- Put down the largest deposit you can because the larger the deposit, the smaller the 'Loan to Value' ratio and the lower interest rate you will pay
- Borrow over the shortest term possible (remembering that you can overpay your mortgage by a certain amount without penalty (usually by about 10% of the outstanding balance) which can give you the flexibility to bring down your mortgage term through overpayment rather than committing to a fixed higher amount each month
- Don't overstretch yourself by taking out the maximum mortgage you are offered - just because the bank will lend you 5 times your annual income, doesn't mean you should borrow that much
- Consider using a mortgage broker, as they see the best offers (some only available to brokers) and take care of the onerous application process for you
- Limit your mortgage payment to a maximum of 30% of your take home pay (aiming for less)
- Always remortgage at the end of your offer period, to reduce the interest you pay and the term where possible

Student loans:

In the UK, student loans don't work in the same way as other loans; there isn't a lump sum borrowed and repaid over time until the debt and interest is fully settled, instead, repayment depends on how much you earn and is written off after a certain period of time. As the cost of University is only increasing, it is important to understand how student loans function and how they play a part in your plans for financial freedom. A summary of the current main student loan plans, including what you repay and the impact on your monthly take home pay (and WBF), is outlined in the table at the end of this chapter (although do check the formal guidance on student loans for the latest position and all available plans[2].

As we will see later, there is correlation between your level of education and your income. Student loans can therefore be viewed more as an investment in an appreciating asset (i.e. yourself) rather than a burdensome debt. Unlike other debts, a student loan doesn't negatively impact your credit score either! That being said, student loan debt reduces your take home pay and consequently reduces the amount you can borrow for other loans and mortgages. Student loans also carry risks, for example, an increase in interest rates and a decrease to the repayment thresholds (the latter requiring Government to pass a bill through the Houses of Parliament, so it is not something done lightly).

If you take out a student loan, another consideration along your financial journey is whether or not to overpay it. When evaluating this, you should consider what returns you can earn elsewhere (either by paying off more expensive debt or investing). If you can earn a higher rate of return than the interest rate on your student loan, it makes sense to avoid over-paying your student loan. If you plan to retire with an income below the repayment threshold at a time before the loan is written off, then any additional funds used to overpay the student loan prior to this, would be a wasted investment.

Summary:
You should now have a good understanding of the different types of debt available to you. As a rule, you should always buy things for cash and only use debt as an absolute

last resort. Debt can be very restrictive for you as it can mean staying in a job you hate, not investing for your future, or even giving up holidays in order to make debt repayments. You will be bombarded with adverts for credit cards, BNPL, car leases, mortgages and personal loans and I urge you to not fall into the trap of just taking what is offered. You should now also understand the methods and implications of borrowing money and I urge you to use this knowledge to make the right financial choices.

Key takeaways:
- Debt comes in many forms, from typical consumer credit used to purchase depreciating assets, to mortgages which underpin an appreciating asset.
- As a general rule you should pay cash wherever possible and only use debt when it is absolutely necessary.
- Do not fall into the trap of trying to impress people by borrowing money to buy nice things!
- Use interest free balance transfers to consolidate credit card debts into one place to help stabilise balances, making them easier to clear.
- Only take out loans if you absolutely have to in order to cover costs of absolute essentials; loans should never be used to purchase 'wants'.
- You can use a credit card for the reward points if it is for a service you regularly use anyway, as long as you pay it off in full every month so you don't incur any interest.
- Don't go into debt to buy or lease a car, save up and buy a reasonable car for cash.
- Follow the golden rules when it comes to mortgages: put down the largest deposit possible over the

shortest term, limiting your mortgage payments to a maximum of 30% of your take-home income.
- Whilst there are risks attached to a student loan, overall, it should be viewed as an investment in yourself.
- Due to the unique nature of student loans, whether or not you direct any of your WBF towards overpaying your student loan debt should be carefully considered.
- Below is a summary of the main student loan plans at the time of writing.

Item	Plan 1	Plan 2	Plan 4
Eligibility	-English or Welsh student on an undergraduate course in the UK before 1/9/2012 -NI undergraduate or postgraduate student in UK on or after 1/9/1998 -EU undergraduate or postgraduate student starting after 1/9/98 but before 1/9/2012	-English or Welsh student who started an undergraduate course in the UK after 1/9/2012 -EU student who started an undergraduate course in England or Wales after 1/9/2012	-Scottish students who started a degree in the UK on or after 1/9/1998
When repayments start	When you have graduated and earning sufficient income		
Interest rate applied	Lower of the Retail Price Index or the Bank of England base rate plus 1%	Whilst studying, Retail Price Index plus up to 3%, upon graduation: - if earning less than £27,295, RPI plus 1.5% - if earning between £27,996 and £49,130, RPI plus 0.15% for every £1,000, capped at 3% - if earning above £49,130, RPI plus 3%	Lower of the Retail Price Index or the Bank of England base rate plus 1%
Interest accrued	Monthly from the date you receive the loan until it is repaid in full or cancelled	Monthly from the date you receive the loan until it is repaid in full or cancelled	Monthly from the date you receive the loan until it is repaid in full or cancelled
Repayment terms	Repay 9% above a monthly pre-tax salary threshold of £1,657 (£19,895 annually)	Repay 9% above a monthly pre-tax salary threshold of £2,274 (£27,288 annually)	Repay 9% above a monthly pre-tax salary threshold of £2,083 (£25,000 annually)
When the loan is written off	After 25 years in the April following graduation if you started University in the 2006/07 academic year or at age 65 if before	30 years after the first April following graduation	Either at age 65 or 30 years after the April following graduation if you started studying on or before the 2006/07 academic year.
Illustration using a £30,000 annual salary	Payment due on £10,105 (£30,000 - £19,895) Pay 9% of £10,105 = £909.45	Payment due on £2,712 (£30,000 - £27,288) Pay 9% of £2,712 = £244.08	Payment due on £5,000 (£30,000 - £25,000) Pay 9% of £5,000 = £450

All about pensions

You may yawn at the prospect of reading about pensions, but it is one of the most important subjects in personal finance, so I plead with you to not skip over this chapter. A pension will likely be someone's biggest financial asset, along with their house, but because you only draw your pension in your older years, it is often an afterthought when you are younger; something 'I'll get to later'. This is a costly error.

A pension is a fund into which you deposit money throughout your working life (often supported by contributions from your employer) and its sole purpose is to provide you with income during your retirement.

A pension is key element in your financial freedom journey: the more money you contribute to your pension earlier on in your career, the quicker you will be able to quit the rat race and re-claim your time back. Because your pension is inaccessible to you until you are at least 55 (at the time of writing, rising to 57 from 2028), it won't be your main source of income if you decide to retire before then, thus the importance of having a separate investment portfolio. Your pension does however provide you with options if you are seeking to retire early. Knowing that you have contributed fully to your pension gives you comfort that you will receive sufficient income in your later life, thereby opening up the opportunity to coast towards retirement, perhaps changing career, reducing your working hours, or becoming self-employed to earn money. The income you can access from a pension later in life provides a safety blanket, enabling you to take some more risk or live life more on your terms, so it is vital to maximise its benefit to you.

In this chapter, we will consider the different types of pension available, along with their respective pros and cons, as well as the main options and key considerations when you come to start withdrawing income from your pension.

Defined benefit pension scheme:
Also known as a 'final salary' scheme, the defined benefit pension scheme was once the most common form of pension. It involves receiving a pre-determined percentage of your salary at your retirement age and each year for the rest of your life. For example, if you earned a £25,000 salary and your scheme paid you 60% of your final salary, you would be guaranteed a £15,000 salary each year from your retirement date until the day you die.

The benefits of this are clear: you have certainty over your income, making financial planning much easier, and, as you tend to earn more money towards the end of your career, your retirement income can be maximised. That said, in order to qualify for the maximum pension, there is a requirement to work for the same employer for a certain number of years (which varies employer to employer). This can have the effect of 'trapping' you in a job you don't like, in order to rack up the years' service required to earn your desired retirement income. Because the population is living longer, the liabilities of defined benefit pension schemes are increasing without sufficient corresponding contributions, or market returns, to help offset them. As a result, the popularity of final salary schemes amongst employers has declined such that they are a rarity in the private sector. They can still be found in the public sector and are, in fact, a key selling point of working in the public sector.

Defined contribution pension scheme:

A defined contribution pension scheme is the most popular pension scheme and is likely to be the one offered to new employees joining the workforce. These schemes involve an employee contributing a certain percentage of their income each month to a pension, with their employer also contributing to the pension in varying degrees, sometimes even matching the employee's contribution. The level of pension-matching varies depending on the employer but it is important to take advantage of an employer's maximum match as it is effectively free money and provides you with a 100% return.

Unlike the defined benefit pension scheme which guarantees you a retirement income based on tenure and final salary, with defined contribution, your retirement income is dependent on the value of your pension fund when you retire; the more you have in your fund, the higher your income. Your retirement is therefore dependent on the value of both yours and your employer's contributions, the investment returns you generate, the fees of your pension provider, and the length of time the money is invested.

As the onus to take care of one's retirement is now on you as an employee rather than your employer, you have the option to select how your pension fund is invested and the ability to change this if you desire to take on more or less risk in order to achieve your desired retirement income. It is now more likely, and common, that you will have several employers during your career and, as such, it is important to keep track of your pension pots and potentially combine them if the costs of doing so don't outweigh the benefits.

Accessing your employer pension:

The rules for accessing pensions do change regularly so it is best to check closer to the relevant time but, as of 2021, you can take 25% of your pension fund as a tax-free lump sum from age 55. This 25% tax-free lump sum can be used for whatever you desire. For example, you could invest it separately, pay off your debts or mortgage, pay for home renovation, pay for your child's University, go on that dream holiday, or buy that nice red Porsche you always wanted… You get the idea. It should be noted that you can take 100% of your pension as a cash lump sum, but this is generally not considered a wise decision as you are likely to face a large tax bill and, if you are not restrained, you could drain your pension fund way too early and scupper your retirement plans. Needless to say, it is vital that you consider your wider financial position and personal circumstances before you make any decisions.

With regards to the remainder of your pension fund, there are two key options available: (1) to buy an annuity; or (2) to go into drawdown.

Buying an annuity:

It used to be very popular to buy an annuity for your retirement and it involves handing your pension fund over to an insurance company who, in return, will provide you with a guaranteed income until you die. This guaranteed income makes your retirement planning easier giving you certainty over your income, which can remove a lot of stress and anxiety in retirement. However, due to the current low interest rate environment, the annual income tends to be quite low and could therefore impact your lifestyle expectations. To get an idea of annuity rates and how much income you could receive, I would suggest looking online at an 'annuity calculator' and researching the various providers and options available to you.

The product offerings within the annuity market are expanding to allow for different personal circumstances. Traditionally, annuities offer a fixed income which can be eroded by inflation over time. As such, to reduce inflation risk, it is now possible to purchase an annuity whose annual income increases by either a set percentage or the prevailing rate of inflation that year, to keep your purchasing power equal, however, this does incur a premium. There are other varieties available, and the market will continue to evolve, so it is best to consult an Independent Financial Adviser when you are approaching retirement if you want to go down this route.

One of the main drawbacks of annuities is that once you pass away, you lose your pension, and your loved ones get nothing. For instance, if you exchanged a £100,000 pension fund for an annuity paying an annual income of £5,000 and lived for 10 years, you would have earned only £50,000 and be out of pocket. Of course the flip side is also true; the longer you live and the more income you get paid, the more value you receive from an annuity, so, if you exchanged a £100,000 pension fund for an annuity paying an annual income of £5,000 and lived for 30 years, you would have earned

£150,000 and be £50,000 in profit.

Going into drawdown:

The alternative to purchasing an annuity is to enter drawdown. This involves leaving your pension invested and extracting income, or 'drawing down', as and when you need it. This option is becoming more popular as people prefer to have the flexibility during retirement to adjust their income as and when required. Having the flexibility to leave your pension invested also gives compound interest time to continually work its magic and grow in value further, potentially giving you a higher income in later years. For example, instead of withdrawing money from your £500,000 pension fund at 60, if you could wait until age 75 and earn a 5% annual return, your portfolio would be worth over £1m(!), so long as you are able to financially support yourself in the meantime. The longer you wait before you access your pension, the more valuable it will be. Drawdown does require you to have a good understanding of investing, as you will be the one responsible for deciding where to invest your money.

Unlike with an annuity, one of the benefits of drawdown is that once you die, any money remaining is not lost and instead can be passed to your heirs as part of your estate. It could, of course, be subject to inheritance tax, so it is best to consider your options as part of wider estate planning with an Independent Financial Adviser.

It is important to remember that regardless of whether you choose an annuity or drawdown option, any income outside of your tax-free lump sum, will be taxed at your marginal income tax rate and you therefore need to consider your pension within the wider context of your estate and other income.

* * *

Self-Invested Personal Pension (SIPP):

Another tax efficient way to save for retirement is in a SIPP. A SIPP is often advised as being something to pay into if you want to increase your pension over and above your employer pension (i.e. from the point your employer no longer matches your contributions). A SIPP is an account in which an individual can make their own decisions as to where they invest their money for retirement. There are several investments not otherwise available in traditional pensions, such as commercial property, unlisted shares, and derivatives, which you can add to your SIPP, as well as traditional investments such as equities and unit trusts; this makes a SIPP an effective tool for sophisticated investors.

Tax relief is available on deposits into a SIPP at your marginal income tax rate; an amount equal to 20% of the deposit amount is automatically added to your account and any difference between the 20% and your income tax rate can be claimed back via your tax return. As with the defined contribution pension scheme, you can access your SIPP from 55 years old (increasing to 57 from 2028) when you can take 25% tax free and the remainder as a drawdown (taxed at your marginal income tax rate) or to buy an annuity. SIPPs are a more sophisticated means to investing and are, typically, only suggested for individuals who are comfortable with managing their own investments. Again, as you can only access your SIPP at a later stage of life, it is not the best investment vehicle if you want to retire earlier.

Individual Savings Accounts (ISAs):

Whilst not exclusively a retirement investment vehicle, the ISA, more specifically the Stocks and Shares ISA, can be used as a key part of your pension planning as it is a tax efficient wrapper in which you can purchase a variety of investments. There are 'target retirement funds' available which behave like your employer pension fund, automatically adjusting the asset allocation within your fund depending on your anticipated retirement date.

The main benefit of a Stocks and Shares ISA, is that any capital growth or income you take from it is tax free no matter the value. There is also a lot of flexibility with an ISA as compared to retirement investment vehicles, as you can access your funds at any age.

In terms of drawbacks, (i) unlike with a SIPP, there is no up-front tax relief, meaning you contribute to your ISA with after tax income, and (ii) there is a maximum annual contribution limit (£20,000 as of the tax year 21/22). Otherwise, a Stocks and Shares ISA is one of the best and most tax efficient instruments available to you.

State Pension:
This is the income you get from the government from age 66 (at the time of writing) and is based on the number of years you have contributed National Insurance to Her Majesty's Treasury. Unfortunately, to date, there has been a skewed perception amongst the general public that the State Pension is sufficient to singlehandedly sustain the population through their retirement years and, consequently, a reliance on the State Pension as the sole source of retirement income. In 2021, the full State Pension offers just over £9,000 per year; barely offering enough to live a very basic life and this is based on 35 years of National Insurance contributions! The UK is undergoing a shift in the population dynamics with people living longer than ever and the number of people in the workforce expected to reduce over time as a result. It is

my prediction that the State Pension will either not be available in 40 years' time or, if it is, it will be severely reduced. In the interest of prudence throughout my financial planning, I always assume that there is not going to be a State Pension available to me for my retirement. If there is, then great, I can treat it like a bonus and use it to travel more, upgrade to business class or stay in 5, instead of 4, star hotels, or provide some extra financial help to family members.

You cannot afford to be reliant on the government for your retirement, and you need to proactively put yourself in a position where your retirement lifestyle is not compromised if the State Pension is not an available option.

Attitude to pensions:

Everybody will have a different idea of what retirement means to them. Some people may want to continue working until the UK State Pension age and then quit work altogether and others may want to retire earlier or later on in their life. As well as desired age of retirement, the desired level of income for retirement is also a personal choice, with some people wanting luxury travel and high end dining as a staple, and others content with staying at home and living a very basic lifestyle. The common denominator when it comes to retirement goals is not *having* to work.

It is vital that you define what retirement looks like for you, in order to help you plan financially; the more specific you can be, the better. For instance, *'I want to have an income of £35,000 per annum, eat out twice per week, go on three long haul holidays per year and have a golf membership'*. The targeted income level should be enough to support the lifestyle you want, and there are numerous online resources available which can help you set realistic goals.[1] Some general guidance from 2020:

- a 'basic' lifestyle, which does not include any holidays, leisure activities or alcohol, cost a single person c.£12,500 per year (c.£17,200 for a couple)
- a 'comfortable' lifestyle, which includes basic European travel, some leisure activities and alcohol, cost a single person c.£19,000 (c.£25,000 for a couple)
- a 'luxurious' lifestyle, which includes some long haul travel, a brand new car every 5 years, as well expensive meals out, health club memberships and charitable giving, cost a single person c.£30,000 (c. £40,000 for a couple).

The difference in retirement funds required for each of these lifestyles (assuming, in each case, you drawdown 4% of your portfolio per year) is as follows: a 'basic' lifestyle with an income of £12,500 per year would require a pension fund of £312,500; a 'comfortable' lifestyle with an income of £19,000 would require a pension fund of £475,000; and a 'luxurious' lifestyle with an income of £30,000 would require a pension fund of £750,000.

Be realistic about the lifestyle you want and whether it is achievable given your current income. For example, if your current annual income is £15,000, it is extremely unlikely that you will save enough into your retirement fund to have a 'luxurious' lifestyle upon retirement. Deciding your future early gives you the best chance of taking the appropriate steps towards achieving your long-term goals.

It is also important to consider the impact of inflation on your retirement income; £30,000 in 2020 is worth less than £30,000 in 2050. The way to feed this into your calculations is by adjusting your annual investment returns by deducting inflation. For example, if the annual investment return is stated as being 6% per year before inflation, the 'real' return you would earn (i.e. the value of your pension fund in today's money) is 6% - 2% = 4%. Let's look at an example: if you were to contribute £1,000 per month (£12,000 per annum) into a pension fund for 30 years and earn 6% per annum, your pension fund would be valued at just over £1m, providing an annual income of £40,000. But if inflation was 2% throughout this period, that annual income of £40,000 would be worth an equivalent of c.£27,000 in today's money.

It should be highlighted that retirement planning is not an exact science and is something that you should undertake a review of regularly. Because your retirement plan is based on a set of circumstances and assumptions and, like everything in life, circumstances change, returns change, and inflation changes, it is important that your future plans always reflect your latest assumptions. For example, the retirement lifestyle you envisage for yourself when you are 25 years old will likely be very different to that when you are 45 years old, be that due to having more or less children than expected, your health not being what you thought, or because you have earned more than you anticipated. All of these factors (along with many others) could influence the amount of money you need in retirement and this emphasises the importance of reviewing your plans regularly.

Another important reason for defining your retirement goals and undertaking your retirement planning early, is that it can help you to avoid assuming more risk than you may be comfortable with (or can actually afford to take). If you were to find out just 5 years before your planned retirement that you are going to have an income shortfall and are not at that point in a position to increase your pension contributions, you will have to make your money work harder by investing in riskier assets (such as emerging market equities). This could be completely against your risk tolerance and mean a bumpy ride into retirement or, in fact, that you have to work much longer than you expected.

Pensions are often seen as dull and boring and something to be taken care of later on in life but, the reality is, we are living longer and need income to support us in our retirement. Try to see your pension as taking care of your future self; the more you can stash away earlier, the longer your money can work for you, rather than you having to work for money. For example, if by age 45 you have £200,000 in pension savings then, assuming an average real return of 5% per year, you can be comfortable that by age 67 you would have almost £585,000 of pension savings, enough to provide an income of £23,000 per annum, sufficient for a comfortable retirement even if you never paid another penny into the fund. Building up a pension fund early opens up numerous opportunities to live a different life, one that is more closely aligned to your values rather than having to continue to trade your time for money indefinitely.

Help out your future self; deal with your pension as early as possible and let your money do the hard work for you. You will be eternally grateful and proud of your younger self for doing so.

Summary:

There are numerous pension options available to help you save for retirement but, whichever you choose, the overwhelming principle you need to grasp is that the more and earlier you invest, the easier your retirement will be and the earlier you are likely to become financially free. Maximise your employer contributions where possible and utilise a Stocks and Shares ISA, or SIPP, for additional retirement savings. When the time comes to withdraw your money, it is best to seek advice from an Independent Financial Adviser as they can offer formal advice on the most tax efficient and appropriate way to access your pension savings.

A brief introduction to investing

Investing is crucial if you are going to achieve financial freedom. Investing means your money will start making money, eventually providing you with enough passive income to enable you to leave the rat race. Investing is a very broad topic and this chapter will explore the various financial markets and the different types of financial instrument available for trading on these markets.

You may be familiar with depositing your savings in a traditional bank savings account, achieving a return of anywhere between 0.1% and, if you're very lucky, 3% depending on how much and for how long you lock your money away. Earning a return of this magnitude will not make you wealthy which is why, as you will find out, I recommend only using these standard savings accounts to house your emergency fund.

In order to have a material, positive, impact on your wealth, you need to expose your savings to the financial markets through investing. Although this may sound intimidating (Wall Street designs it this way), once you understand the principles, you will realise it's not so complex and your confidence will grow exponentially.

* * *

Financial markets available to investors:
Stock markets:

When you hear the term 'financial markets', you probably think of the 'stock market' but the stock market is only one of a number of markets. The stock market is primarily the place companies sell ownership stakes in their company; their 'Equity' (or 'share' of a business). Businesses raise money for a variety of reasons, whether this be to expand the business through the building of a new factory, opening more shops, launching a digital sales channel, developing a new product or even paying off debts.

There are two broad classifications of stock markets: *developed* and *emerging*. 'Developed' markets are those situated in the world's most economically developed countries and are outlined below with the names of their respective stock market indexes:

- **UK**: FTSE 100 (the biggest 100 companies in the UK by value), FTSE 250 (the next 250 biggest companies in the UK)
- **USA**: S&P 500 (the 500 largest companies in the USA by value) NASDAQ, (this is the technology focused index)
- **Japan**: Nikkei 225 (the top 225 companies in Japan by value)
- **Germany**: Xetra DAX (the top 30 companies in Germany by value)
- **France**: Paris CAC 40 (largest 40 companies in France by value)
- **Hong Kong**: Hang Seng (the largest 50 companies in Hong Kong by value)

* * *

The fact a company is listed on a particular stock market doesn't necessarily mean its sales and profits are only earned in that jurisdiction, in fact, it is quite the opposite, with most of these companies' operations and sales being truly global.

The developed markets are a cornerstone of an investment portfolio and buying into them is akin to owning a small part of each of the largest companies in the world. These markets tend to have average annual returns of around 8% (much better than your savings account), but with this, comes risk and there is volatility where markets have lost (in the worst years) 30%-50% of their value (such as during the financial crises in 2008/09 and the COVID-19 pandemic).

'Emerging' markets are those economies which are yet to establish themselves as global powerhouses but, with that, comes huge opportunities for growth. These economies tend to have younger populations, less established governments and be relatively new to the free market system. Some examples include China, Eastern Europe, Brazil, India, Vietnam and Indonesia (to name but a few). As you might expect, there is a reward for investing in the higher risk emerging markets, as they average an annual return of just under 11%;[1] you get compensated for adopting the additional risk. I will explain how to invest in these markets in more detail later on, but they should form part of your investment portfolio if you want (or need) to increase your returns in order to achieve your financial objectives.

As stock markets tend to be volatile, and this volatility is widely publicised in the newspapers and reported on the news channels, it makes them seem a very risky investment and something to be avoided. Admittedly, the stock markets do rise and fall daily but investing is a long term game and over time the markets grow. My view is that you are taking as big of a risk by not investing, as your money is eroding in value due to inflation.

Bond markets:

As well as selling shares to fund business expansion, companies also raise money by borrowing money from investors. They do this by issuing bonds, essentially 'IOUs' repayable over time with a pre-defined interest rate (which we will cover in more detail later on).

As at 2021, the global bond market was worth in the region of USD 119 trillion[2] (or in long hand USD 119,000,000,000,000!) and covers debt issued by companies as well as governments. To put the sheer size of the bond market into perspective, the total value of all the goods and services produced and sold throughout the global economy is worth USD 87 trillion. The bond market is, simply, huge. Bonds are generally split into 'Government' and 'Corporate' bonds which are sub-divided into 'investment grade' or 'junk' (essentially, 'non-investment grade'). Junk bonds, as you might infer from the terminology, are higher risk but, consequently, carry a higher return.

Bonds should form a fair percentage (about 20-40%) of a well-balanced investment portfolio. They provide a steady income and their prices tend to move in a different and opposite direction to equities and so act as a ballast in a portfolio in times of significant volatility and can help ensure capital is preserved.

Foreign exchange (FX / FOREX) markets:

If you have ever been on holiday and had to exchange your currency, you have accessed the foreign exchange (also known as 'Forex' or 'FX') market. The FX market is simply massive with daily(!) transaction volumes of USD 5 trillion. It is used by everyone; from individual speculators trying to profit from buying and selling volatile currencies, to massive multinational companies who use it to hedge their foreign currency payments and receipts, and even holiday makers buying currency for spending money abroad. FX markets will not be a core element of achieving your financial freedom and it is important that you ignore any advertisement claiming 'people got rich overnight by speculating on currency', or 'have a 'FX trading system' which can make you millions'. These adverts are simply misleading and should be avoided at all costs; you work too hard for your money to lose it to speculative trading systems. My opinion? Ignore them, and just use the FX markets for converting your currency when going on holiday.

Commodities markets:

The raw materials used to produce all the goods we consume are bought and sold on the commodities markets. There are about 100 markets worldwide where the prices of oil, grain, pork, gold, silver, iron ore, copper, cocoa, coffee and many more raw materials are set through the power of supply and demand, which influences the prices for everything from fuelling our homes and cars to our weekly grocery shop. Commodities markets work by offering buyers the chance to buy raw materials at a fixed price today, for delivery at a future date. This is an instrument known as a 'futures contract' and helps (i) producers of commodities gain certainty over their sale prices, and (ii) the users of commodities achieve certainty over their costs of production. The main index for commodities is the 'GSCI Commodities Index' which tracks the price of a basket of commodities across energy, livestock, agricultural and precious and industrial metals.

* * *

Commodities can be an important element of investment strategy as they provide an extra layer of diversification, which can reduce the overall risk of a portfolio. Like with bond investing, you will not purchase individual futures contracts for each commodity (unless you want 100 tons of coffee beans delivered to your house in three months' time!) but buy funds which themselves invest in these contracts in order to track the index and companies that produce these resources.

Property markets:

You will be familiar with the property market if you have ever bought or rented a property. When you rent, you give the owner of the property an income; and when you own, you will, hopefully, see the value of your property increase. There are various other forms of property market including commercial property (which incorporates office space, shopping centres, shops etc.), residential property (the one we are most familiar with) and industrial property (storage units, containers, warehouses etc.)

The property market is less liquid than the other markets (just think of how long it takes to buy or sell a house) and is not actively traded on an exchange, which means there can be opportunities to earn substantial returns. A standard way of getting exposure to property is by buying a second property which you rent out for income ('buy to let') or buying a stake in an office building. However, this kind of investment requires deep pockets to form even a small part of an investment portfolio.

There is a solution to this illiquid property market and this comes in the form of 'Real Estate Investment Trusts' (REITs).

REITs are companies, whose shares are listed on stock exchanges, that only invest in large portfolios of property and provide income to investors through dividends. REITs can give the everyday investor exposure to the property market, without requiring hundreds of thousands of pounds of personal investment.

Types of investment instrument available to an investor:

With an understanding of the key financial markets under your belt, the next step, covered by this chapter, is to understand the specific instruments that can be purchased as investments from the financial markets.

Equities:

Equities, also known as 'stocks' or 'shares', give you an ownership stake in a business along with certain rights. Large companies known as 'Public Limited Companies' or 'PLCs' issue shares on the stock exchange for public and professional investors to purchase and it is recommended that these make up the majority of your investment portfolio.

Owning equity in a business gives you a right to receive a share of its future profits in the form of dividends and allows you to vote on certain matters such as issuing new shares and director incentive plans. It is important to remember though that a company doesn't have to pay a dividend, it is at the discretion of the Board of Directors. This is unlike interest on bonds, the payment of which is compulsory.

Shares are also issued by smaller companies known as 'private limited' or 'ltd' companies but these are not generally available for sale to the public. Limited company shares are common with owner managed businesses which we will explore further in the 'Side Hustle' chapter. You do not need to worry about including these in your investment portfolio unless you are seeking to take significant risk to boost returns in the long term or have significant control over the business.

Investors receive a return on equities in two ways: i) share price increases (capital gains); and ii) dividends. What causes share prices to rise and fall is beyond the scope of this book but the main point to note is that, over the long term, the value of a business will typically rise. That said, as they are exposed to the business cycle of boom/bust and shocks such as COVID-19, the prices can be volatile. You need to have the capacity and discipline to leave your money invested long term (think 10 plus years) and the stomach to not panic sell when you experience paper losses due to such volatility as, although it is unpleasant, it is unlikely to be permanent (it is only permanent if you sell). Underneath every share price is a business, buying and selling products and services, that has employees, suppliers and customers, and it is unlikely to fundamentally change from one day to the next to justify some of the wild swings in price you will see on the stock market.

You can invest in equities by buying individual shares, but I would not recommend this to the vast majority of investors as it is risky, costly and requires you to actively manage a portfolio of individual companies which can feel like a full time job (in fact this is a career in its own right). My view is that only experts should be buying individual shares. The rest of us should look to build an investment portfolio made up of well diversified, cheap, index funds in order to spread risk whilst earning the market return.

If, however, you do decide to buy individual equities, you can do this through a stock broker or brokerage account.

You'd see two relevant prices - the 'bid' and 'offer'. The bid price is the price you'd receive if you sold your shares; and the offer price is the price you'd pay to buy them. The difference between the two prices is the 'spread' which is the commission the brokers earn and is unavoidable. You would also pay a trading fee (which varies, but can be up to £15 depending on the provider) and a Stamp Duty Reserve Tax (SDRT) of 0.5% (assuming you buy online).

A common mistake people make when investing is that they invest a significant percentage of their savings in their employer's shares. They perceive this to be a safe option because they work for the company but they are effectively taking a one way bet on their employer. There have been countless companies go bankrupt and retirement plans blown apart due to the often unthinkable happening. Remember Blockbuster, Enron, Kodak and Lehman Brothers? Nobody ever thought that these companies would capitulate. As such, diversification across a number of companies, industries and investment instruments is crucial to spread your risk. I am not saying don't buy into your employer's share scheme, after all, they often offer valuable discounts for doing so. What I am saying is that you should ensure any such investment is part of a broader, diverse, investment portfolio.

Bonds:
Bonds are issued by companies and governments in order to raise cash. By buying bonds, investors are essentially lending money to the relevant company or government in exchange for, on average, a return of around 5% per year.[3]

Every bond issuer is given a credit rating by an agency such as S&P, Moody's or Fitch. Such credit ratings range from the top rating 'AAA' ('triple A') to the lowest rating 'D' ('in default') and are broadly categorised into 'investment' and 'non-investment' grades. As a general rule, the higher the credit rating the more likely the issuer will be to pay investors the interest due on their bonds and repay their principal, and, consequently, the lower the return will be on the investment, (and vice versa).

So how do bonds work?

Each bond has a face value of £100. A bond can be bought at par (for £100), at a discount (for less than £100), or at a premium (for more than £100) and an interest payment, which is a percentage of the face value known as the Coupon, is paid semi-annually or annually. Regardless of the price you pay for a bond, the amount repaid to you by the bond issuer at the end of the term will always be the face value price of £100. As such, the purchase price you pay for bonds will heavily impact your total return (or 'yield to maturity' in bond language). Unsurprisingly, there is correlation between the credit rating of an issuer and the price of their bonds: the lower the credit rating, the cheaper the bond, and the higher the return. As is a common theme of investing, you are compensated with higher returns for taking additional risk.

Bonds are best understood with an example. Consider a 5 year bond bought at par (for £100) paying a 3% annual coupon.

Each year from year 1 to year 4, you would receive £3 (3% of £100) in interest on the bond, and at the end year 5 you would receive £103 (your £3 interest plus the repayment of the £100 principal). So, from your £100 investment you receive £115 after 5 years. You can see the appeal of bonds as an instrument to provide a consistent, safe and passive income.

* * *

A drawback of bonds is that they are negatively impacted by inflation. As the return is fixed into the future, if actual inflation is higher than it was initially expected at the time you bought the bond, the 'real' value of the interest payment is reduced. There are, however, inflation-linked bonds whose coupons do increase in line with inflation in order to negate this risk.

So, who are bonds for? In terms of buying these instruments, individual bonds are only available to high net worth individuals (usually those with a minimum investment of £50,000) or investment and pension funds. The method of buying bonds available to the rest of us is to utilise investment funds and Exchange Traded Funds ('ETFs'). ETFs are arguably one of the best inventions in finance and have really opened up the financial markets to the public. These funds allow individuals to invest in not individual bonds but a pool of bonds from as little as £100.

Exchange Traded Funds (ETFs), sometimes called 'Index Funds':

ETFs are passively managed, generally computerised, investment vehicles. They invest in all the components (e.g. companies, bonds, commodities) of an underlying index and have the benefit of automatic rebalancing to ensure that the price of the fund follows the movements of the underlying index. Again, to understand ETFs, it is helpful to look at an example. A 'FTSE 100 Index Fund', as an ETF, would own shares in every FTSE 100 company, in the same weightings of the FTSE 100 index. As a result of such weightings, the price of such FTSE 100 Index Fund would mirror that of the whole FTSE 100 index. Whilst the principles of ETFs can be overwhelming, even off-putting, at first, there are so many benefits to using ETFs in your investment portfolio which make understanding them worthwhile. Such benefits include:

- ✓ **Low cost** - you don't need to pay to trade ETFs. There is however an annual fee of around 0.1% - 0.5% depending on the index and provider but this is a small price to pay to expose your money to the markets. For instance, you can buy a FTSE 100 index tracker for less than 0.1% in annual fees and this is something that has returned an average of just under 9% per year for the last 35 years!![4]
- ✓ **Diversified** – investing in an index fund will mean you own every investment available on the relevant market. As such, you reduce the risk of losing your money that is associated with exposing yourself to buying individual shares.
- ✓ **Varied** - there is an ETF for every market you could think of, from the core financial market indices to specific sub-sections of markets such as technology, environment, high yield, high growth, small companies, large companies, etc.
- ✓ **Tailored portfolio** - you can dial your exposure to different markets up or down by investing across a variety of ETFs. For instance, you could invest in equities in the UK, USA, Japan, Europe and Emerging Markets and add a global bond ETF in whatever proportion you like to suit your risk tolerance and ensure you are best placed to meet your objectives.
- ✓ **Off the shelf portfolio** - there are funds available which enable you to buy a ready-made, diversified portfolio which require zero effort to manage. For example, Vanguard's Life Strategy funds provide a portfolio with pre-determined asset allocations (e.g.

60% equities, 40% bonds) that is automatically rebalanced, for a very small annual fee.
✓ **Liquid** - the market for ETFs is massive, meaning you can buy and sell at minimal spreads and very quickly; you can buy ETFs instantly and can have your cash back within a few days if you decide to sell.

What are the drawbacks?, you may ask. The main one, is that you will only ever match, and never beat, the returns of the market, but, quite frankly, even the professionals never really beat the market consistently (especially when fees are considered) and you will be doing so much better from ETFs vs just parking your hard earned money in a savings account.

Investment funds:

An alternative to buying passively managed index funds, is to invest in 'actively managed' funds. This is the approach taken by hedge funds and mutual funds and involves having a fund manager (and their team) researching and devising strategy on which shares, bonds and commodities to buy and sell in the portfolio, with the sole aim of beating the market (or earning 'alpha' in industry terms).

The benefit of an actively managed fund is that you can beat the market return if you select the right investment managers. This is because active managers are often presented with more adventurous opportunities; high growth, unlisted companies approach hedge funds and private equity houses for investment (whereas such companies are not available for passive investing).

There are however several drawbacks to investing in actively managed funds:

- Only a small percentage (18%) of fund managers beat the market over a sustained period[5]
- As there tends to be a lot of buying and selling in the pursuit of generating excess returns, dealing costs begin to add up and these are passed on to the investor in the form of management fees and fund expenses which can be anywhere between 1% and 5%, denting your returns
- There is sometimes a performance fee on top of the cost of the fund e.g. a 20% fee on any gain over a certain benchmark, again costing the investor more
- There are inconsistencies in the funds that beat the market, so it's hard to pick winners every time

As with investing in individual shares, I would suggest extensively researching actively managed investment funds and regularly monitoring their performance to ensure the relevant investment is performing the way you intended and deserving of a place in your portfolio. Actively managed investment funds can be a good way of trying to generate some additional return in a small part (or 'satellite') of your portfolio but I would not suggest investing all your money in such funds due to the fees eating away at your return and the high likelihood that they won't beat the market return you would otherwise achieve by investing in passive funds over time.

Summary:

Your journey to financial freedom will require you to invest in financial markets in one way or another and you should embrace index funds as much as possible to give you a cheap way of building a diversified portfolio. All you then have to do is: concentrate on investing regularly; keep your nerve and not sell during market volatilities; and keep going, letting time and compound interest work its magic.

Key takeaways:
- Global financial markets are comprised of: stock markets (broadly categorised into developed and emerging); bond markets; commodities markets; foreign exchange markets; and property markets.
- Shares, bonds, commodities and property will be key investments on your path to financial freedom.
- The cheapest and most efficient method of investing in the financial markets is through Exchange Traded Funds (ETFs), also known as index funds, which track the movement of the underlying index.
- Alternatively, there is an option to invest in actively managed investment funds (which employ professionals to try and beat the market). You should exercise caution before investing in actively managed investment funds, as you are highly unlikely to outperform a basic ETF/index fund.

Approaches to investing

The previous chapter explained how the financial markets work and the types of products available for purchase. This chapter will explain how you can approach investing with the goal of giving you the confidence to build your own investment portfolio. *'What's the incentive to do that?'*, you ask. The returns from your investments will ultimately be a source of income to support you in your retirement. *'Retirement? Well, I already pay into a pension so, thanks, but I'm covered.'* It is a common misconception that retirement is something that you enter at a State-determined age (currently between 66 and 68, depending on one's year of birth). My view, however, is that retirement is not an age, rather a number in your 'bank account'; put simply, you can retire when you have enough money to live the lifestyle you want without needing to work in order to do so. This is what keeps me focussed and investing aggressively. *'That sounds good!'* Great, please keep reading.

How to approach investing:

As outlined in the previous chapter, there are ready made portfolios which can be purchased off the shelf and allow you to invest in a diversified portfolio with minimal effort, such as Vanguard's Life Strategy funds.

***

Should you want to take a more active approach in managing your investments yourself rather than via investment funds, there are numerous portfolio management techniques available. The detail of such techniques is well beyond the scope of this book, but there are two general approaches which are easy to follow and implement and are all you need to really know:

- *investing in a basic stock/bond portfolio* - this involves holding a certain percentage of shares and bonds and is designed to earn a diversified return from both the stock and bond markets. Using this technique, an investor would buy a global stock market ETF and global bond ETF in the following proportions: the percentage of shares should be 100 less your age (and the remainder should be invested in bonds). For example, if you are 35, your allocation to stocks would be (100-35) 65% and thus 35% in bonds. The higher the percentage weighting of shares, the higher the return (but the higher the volatility).
- *holding a 'core/satellite' portfolio* - this involves a rough 80/20 split of having 80% of your portfolio made up of 'core' investments which is a selection of diversified funds covering equities, bonds, cash, commodities and property across numerous core markets, and 20% in higher risk investments such as actively managed investment funds, individual shares and emerging markets. The aim of this approach is to earn the market return from your core investments and try to add some additional return by having some more speculative investments in the 'satellite'. This is where actively managed investment funds, smaller company shares and emerging

markets can play a part in your financial plan. As always, you need to be aware of your risk tolerance and capacity to take risk when deciding on your investment selection.

Taking an active approach to your investments gives you full control over how you allocate your money but it does require a deeper understanding of portfolio management, discipline to keep on top of your plans and time to research funds and involves a three step process.

Step one: you need to determine your target asset allocation i.e. what percentage of equities, bonds, cash, commodities, and property you need in your portfolio in order to achieve your investment objectives. This is a very important decision for you, as it determines the rate of return and the level of risk and volatility your portfolio will have. Be too conservative and you could end up missing out on returns; be too risky and you could end up with your portfolio falling in value just at the time you intend to retire early. The higher the weighting of equities in your portfolio, the higher the return but the higher the risk; the higher the weighting of bonds, the lower the risk.

The table below shows the return and annual volatility of portfolios made up of a variety of equity and bond asset allocations, and demonstrates the point that introducing equities increases returns but also adds more risk.

Asset Allocation		% Return				Annual
Equity %	Bond %	1 year	3 year	5 year	10 year	Volatility
100%	0%	26.1%	30.2%	70.1%	182.6%	9.7%
80%	20%	20.4%	27.4%	57.7%	153.3%	7.9%
60%	40%	14.9%	24.3%	45.7%	125.2%	6.3%
40%	60%	9.4%	21.0%	33.9%	98.5%	5.1%
20%	80%	4.5%	18.0%	23.7%	74.5%	4.2%

Source: Vanguard Life Strategy funds, as at July 2021

***

Generally, the further away from retirement you are, the higher your allocation to equities should be, to give you the best chance of maximising your returns. As you approach your financial freedom date, you should reduce the volatility by increasing your proportion of bonds whilst still earning enough to maintain your capital to support the 4% withdrawal per year.

Step two: once you have determined your target asset allocation, you then need to select the funds to include within your portfolio, being careful to select the lowest cost ETF that tracks the underlying index as closely as possible. For example, if you decide you want 60% of your portfolio in equities, you could either buy a single global equities index fund which will track all of the major stock markets, or you could buy several individual market ETFs (such as the USA, UK and German market) to comprise your equity allocation. There is no right or wrong answer as to which markets you include, but having a broad coverage is important to diversify your exposure and help reduce risk.

Step three: the ongoing requirement of actively managing your own portfolio is to monitor the performance, and keep track of the fees, of both your selected funds as well as any similar funds, to ensure you are maximising the value for your money. There is no need to pay 0.2% per year for an ETF to track the FTSE 100 if one that does the same job is available for 0.1%! Expenses compound and act as a parachute, dragging your returns down, so it is important to keep them as small as possible.

With any approach to actively managing your investment portfolio yourself, it is vital to rebalance your portfolio allocations regularly to ensure price movements have not caused your allocations to move so much that it changes the nature of your portfolio, with it becoming too risky or not risky enough. For example, if you set a target asset allocation of 80% equities / 20% bonds at the start of the year but, after one year, equities have underperformed bonds so the allocation is now 70% equities / 30% bonds (meaning your expected returns are now lower than originally anticipated), you need to rebalance your portfolio by selling bonds and buying equities in the proportion that would meet your target allocation.

The frequency of rebalancing your portfolio can vary:
- if you are investing regularly, for instance putting a portion of your monthly salary into your investments, then you can rebalance each time you invest
- if you receive a one off windfall, such as a bonus or inheritance, this is another opportunity to evaluate your allocation and invest in the relevant proportions to maintain your target
- if you are unlikely to contribute any additional income to your portfolio, for example because you have retired early and finally quit the rat race, then consider evaluating your investments every six to twelve months and rebalance as you see fit.

Re-balancing can often seem counter-intuitive as you are buying assets that have gone down in value and selling those that are increasing but what this ensures is that you buy low and sell high which is vital in the unpredictable nature of asset returns, as you will see later in this chapter.

I personally take a more active approach, managing an

investment portfolio comprised mainly of ETFs in the core with some individual shares in the satellite. I like the level of control this affords me as well as the self-education I receive from managing a portfolio. It is time consuming as you need to be on top of your investments and ensure your funds are the most cost effective they can be. Moreover, this approach requires a controlled and disciplined mindset as you will see the value of your investments fluctuate significantly on a regular basis and you cannot give into your emotions and panic sell, as this would undermine your efforts.

Active portfolio management is appropriate if you enjoy actively researching and managing your investment choices and asset allocation but it is not for everyone and should probably be avoided if you do not have this interest. Also, before adopting this approach, I would strongly suggest reading further into investing, asset allocation and portfolio management as knowledge is power when it comes to executing this effectively.

Using a Financial Adviser to manage your investments:

Instead of managing your investments yourself, an alternative is to let a Financial Adviser do this on your behalf. The adviser will evaluate your financial position and construct a portfolio that will help you achieve your objectives. This can be an expensive approach with an initial fee (commonly over £1,000) to create your portfolio and ongoing management fees (often being over 1% of your portfolio value) which you pay on top of the fees of the funds you buy.

If you are keen on this approach, I would recommend using an *Independent* Financial Adviser as they are obliged to operate in your best interest and have access to the entire market when it comes to selecting investments. Non-independent advisers are linked to certain companies and only offer products available from certain providers and so, although they can be a slightly cheaper alternative, the service is limited.

My general view, which I often share with my clients, is that Financial Advisers should be consulted when it comes to complex estate planning such as reducing inheritance tax exposures on large estates in the event of bereavement, rather than for managing a basic investment portfolio which you can easily do yourself.

How to actually go about investing:

In my opinion, the best vehicle through which to invest is a 'Stocks and Shares ISA'. This is a tax efficient wrapper for your investments, which means any capital gains or income is completely tax free. There is an annual allowance limiting the value of contributions, currently £20,000 (in 2021), that is revised each year so you should keep abreast of the allowance and aim to maximise it each year.

There are multiple providers of these ISAs including Vanguard, Hargreaves Lansdown and Legal and General. You are only allowed one, so it is important to research the costs and benefits of the platform against your personal needs. Each provider charges a fee for use of the platform (usually a percentage fee based on the value of your investments) for which there are varying levels of access to investments and research tools which, as you can imagine, vary with the fee.

The more expensive providers (e.g. Hargreaves Lansdown) tend to give you more access to different funds and markets and the cheaper providers (e.g. Vanguard) have more restricted investment choices and limited research tools. It is a personal preference as to which provider to use but I would suggest using a more restricted provider if you want a simpler and more passive approach to investing and one with more research tools if you want to take a more active approach.

Fees do eat into your returns, so it is important that you utilise the full functionality of the platform you choose in order to maximise the cost. For instance, if you opened a Hargreaves Lansdown account and only invested in cheap funds which are otherwise available via cheaper providers, you are wasting your money; you would be better opening an account with Vanguard who only give you access to their own funds.

Investment strategy:

Thousands of investment strategies have been developed and implemented to generate good returns from investment portfolios. Whilst it is beyond the scope of this book to go into the details of these, there are some fundamental concepts and common themes underlying the majority of the strategies, as follows.

Diversify:

You will have heard the phrase 'don't put all of your eggs in one basket' and this is pertinent when it comes to investing. You need to ensure your money is spread across multiple areas, not just different asset classes (equities, bonds, property, commodities etc.) but a variety of assets within these asset classes.

Take equities for example; you should have geographical

diversification by investing in equities across different countries (not just in your home market). This can be ensured by buying index funds for the UK, USA, Japan, and European stock markets or buying into a 'global' equity fund which will invest across a number of key international markets.

The main reason for diversifying is simple: to spread your risk and ensure that your money is not wiped out by a one off event in a certain country or particular company. For example, if you had all of your money invested in your employer's shares and a competitor enters the market with a new product causing your employer to go out of business. If you had diversified and had only a small portion of your money invested in your employer, you wouldn't be in financial ruin as a result of the new competition.

Asset classes also behave in different ways under different economic circumstances creating unpredictable returns. As such, to give yourself the best chance of maximising your returns, it is important to have investments across all asset classes.

The table below shows the annual percentage return across the ten major markets over the last five financial years (from April to March). This highlights the unpredictable nature of returns and importance of having your money exposed to the variety of asset classes.

* * *

Rank	2016-17	2017-18	2018-19	2019-20	2020-21
1st	Europe (ex. UK) (22.09%)	North America (19.51%)	UK Government Bonds (13.63%)	North America (9.02%)	UK All Companies (32.49%)
2nd	Global Emerging Markets (17.84%)	Japan (12.14%)	Global Government Bonds (11.47%)	Asia Pacific (ex. Japan) (7.59%)	North America (26.81%)
3rd	Asia Pacific (ex. Japan) (15.44%)	Global (11.8%)	UK Corporate Bonds (9.04%)	Global (7.38%)	Global (23.79%)
4th	Global (15.01%)	UK All Companies (5.63%)	Global Corporate Bonds (8.6%)	UK Corporate Bonds (4.2%)	Europe (ex. UK) (22.39%)
5th	North America (14.77%)	Asia Pacific (ex. Japan) (4.04%)	Global Emerging Markets (7.3%)	UK Government Bonds (4.07%)	Global Emerging Markets (18.57%)
6th	UK All Companies (13.84%)	Europe (ex. UK) (1.81%)	North America (7.22%)	Japan (3.84%)	Japan (17.47%)
7th	Japan (13.78%)	Global High Yield Bonds (0.86%)	Asia Pacific (ex. Japan) (6.09%)	Global Corporate Bonds (3.82%)	Asia Pacific (ex. Japan) (15.32%)
8th	Global High Yield Bonds (6.77%)	UK Government Bonds (0.63%)	Global High Yield Bonds (6.05%)	Europe (ex. UK) (3.48%)	Global High Yield Bonds (7.9%)
9th	Global Corporate Bonds (1.87%)	UK Corporate Bonds (-0.13%)	Global (5.88%)	Global Emerging Markets (2.05%)	Global Corporate Bonds (2.12%)
10th	UK Corporate Bonds (0.57%)	Global Government Bonds (-0.56%)	Europe (ex. UK) (1.96%)	Global Government Bonds (1.57%)	UK Corporate Bonds (1.3%)
11th	Global Government Bonds (-2.28%)	Global Emerging Markets (-0.76%)	UK All Companies (0.08%)	Global High Yield Bonds (-0.16%)	Global Government Bonds (-4.52%)
12th	UK Government Bonds (-5.73%)	Global Corporate Bonds (-0.95%)	Japan (-1.18%)	UK All Companies (-13.13%)	UK Government Bonds (-7.23%)

Source: Hargreaves Lansdown Investment Times issue 150 - autumn 2021 (Lipper IM) returns calculated from 30/09/16 to 30/09/21

As you can see, the unpredictability of the returns of asset classes indicates the value of diversification. Take Global Emerging Markets for instance, appearing in position 2, 11, 5 and 9 over 5 years! Having exposure to all of these major markets by virtue of a diverse investment portfolio, gives you the upside of the 'winning' assets and minimises the downside of the losing assets.

Buy and hold:

You may be tempted to trade individual stocks quickly in

an attempt to maximise your returns (much like the traders you see in TV dramas and the adverts which seem to infiltrate most YouTube feeds!). However, this strategy does not work for small, private investors due not only to excessive trading fees eating into profits as discussed earlier in this chapter but, more importantly, the fact that you, realistically, don't have enough time to effectively research trading opportunities and actively manage your portfolio in this way. To put it into context, remember, there are full time professional traders working 16 hour days with teams of highly skilled professionals supporting them who can't always make money...

Financial markets are volatile, with prices moving up and down each day depending on news flow, economic data and company financial results. You may think the volatility in the markets offers the opportunity to buy when the market is low and sell when it is high, but nobody can time the market properly and you are therefore more likely to miss out on positive returns by not being in the market than if you were to be selling to avoid the downward market moves. You should invest and leave your money alone, buy and hold, and just forget trying to time the market; if you invest regularly, particularly in managed funds, you will naturally take advantage of the volatility as such funds will buy more units of an ETF when the market falls, thereby bringing down your average holding price.

It is important that you take a long term view when investing. Grow your wealth through consistency and discipline over many years, rather than by speculating on volatile price movements. The golden rule to achieving long term success is to buy and hold your diversified investment portfolio and invest as regularly as you can; time is a friend of investors and, if you can do your best to ignore the daily movements and bad news on financial markets, only reviewing your investments periodically when you seek to rebalance your funds, you'll give yourself the best chance of success.

Reinvest:

One of the most important elements of maximising the return on your investments is earning income in the form of dividends from equity holdings and interest from bonds. It can be very tempting to take this dividend/interest income and go to the pub for a couple of cold pints but I urge you to resist; I cannot emphasise enough the importance of reinvesting this income by buying more of the assets that generated the income for you.

If you still need some persuading, consider the figures in the following example: if you invested £10,000 in the FTSE 100 in 1986 and took your dividends as income, in 2020 your money would be worth just over £53,000. This sounds impressive, but, if you had reinvested your dividends, your investment would be worth almost £196,000 (4 times as much).[1] This is dividend reinvestment and compound interest at its finest!

To practically reinvest your earned dividends, the funds you purchase will often come with an option for 'accumulation' or 'income', the former reinvesting dividends automatically on your behalf, with the latter depositing the cash into your investment account. In addition, your investment platform provider should have the option to have all income paid as cash or automatically reinvested. If you do elect to have income paid into your investment account, you will then need to manually purchase additional investments.

* * *

Review your fund fees regularly:

As mentioned earlier, fees do reduce investment returns so a key element of your investment strategy is to regularly review the fees of each fund you invest in, as well as your platform provider to ensure you are getting good value for money. For example, if you find a FTSE 100 index tracker which costs 0.06% per annum and yours currently costs you 0.15%, you should switch to the cheaper option as both funds do exactly the same; that is, track the performance of the FTSE 100.

Summary:

Investing is essential if you want to achieve financial freedom. Having a disciplined approach to building a well-diversified portfolio using index funds and maintaining a desired asset allocation, gives you a solid foundation to building wealth. Investing is a long term game; avoid trying to time the market, ignore the short term fluctuations of prices, and avoid the temptation of panic selling. Remember, you are investing to build wealth for your future self; you are planting a seed now to have an oak tree later, and you need to keep this in mind. You wouldn't rip out your two metre tall oak tree because it lost its leaves in the winter, so don't do this to your investments.

Key takeaways:
- Two common portfolio construction methods are a simple stock/bond portfolio and a core/satellite method.
- Your portfolio should consist of cheap index funds and cover a broad range of markets to diversify away risk.
- You need to determine your asset allocation and

review your portfolio regularly to ensure it is performing in line with your anticipated allocation and make changes if required.
- Forget about trying to time the market or trading your way to financial freedom, invest as often as you can and keep your money in the market - its *time in* the market that counts, not *timing* the market.
- Review the fees of your investments on a regular basis and don't be afraid to switch provider or fund if you can get the same thing for less.
- Income reinvestment will supercharge your long term rewards - don't spend your dividend or interest income, buy more of the investments that generated this income!

Budgeting techniques

One of the key skills you need if you are to be successful with your finances is, budgeting. This is such a vital skill, and it is criminal that it is not compulsory on the school curriculum. In the coming pages, I will teach you the basics of budgeting and some common techniques. There is no right or wrong approach to budgeting (as long as you do it), so feel free to experiment until you find a method that suits you.

Put simply, a 'budget' is used to instil control in to finances. It is set at a point in time and can be set daily, weekly, monthly, quarterly, annually or across multiple years, and tracks income, expenses, savings and investments. Budgeting may sound dull, boring, time consuming, and complex but it doesn't have to be and the benefits are huge, not just for your bank balance but for your mental health. The causal relationship between money issues and mental health have been well documented and it is well established that the more financial difficulty you are in, the more likely you are to experience mental ill health. According to the charity Money and Mental Health, people with depression and problem debt are 4.2 times more likely to still be depressed 18 months later, and people with problem debt are three times more likely to have had suicidal thoughts in the past year![1] Budgeting is the cornerstone of financial planning and will not only help you financially but could also be life-saving.

Having a budget also puts you back in control of your money; you know where it should go and, as you are in control of your day to day spending, you ensure it goes where it is needed. I strongly believe that without a budget or financial plan, money will be something that intimidates and controls your life and you will never achieve your potential without one.

How to build your budget:

The first step towards building a budget is to set out your financial objective(s) and timing for success. From there, you should work backwards to create smaller financial goals and corresponding timeframes. I, personally, have a 5 year financial plan which sets out the amounts I want to have saved and invested; working backwards, I then have a 1 year budget broken down by month. These shorter term monthly goals enable me to stay on track to achieve my annual and, in turn, my 5 year goal. Your goals should be realistic but challenging. If your monthly income is £2,000, it is no good having an annual savings target of £25,000 as this would be unrealistic and demotivating, but, having a target that is achievable with some discipline, would help to keep you motivated along the way and build momentum as you approach your target.

When preparing your budget, start with your income and then deduct the following: amounts for your wealth building activity (e.g. savings, pensions investment), your essential living costs (e.g. rent/mortgage, utility bills, food, travel), and then, finally, your discretionary spend. You need to allocate every penny of your income so that it has a purpose which aligns to your objectives. Reading this, you might be thinking that I have the order wrong; surely my living costs should be first and I'll save or invest what is left? The reality is that, taking this approach, you won't be maximising your wealth building, you need to live on what is left after saving and investing. I have included a template you could use for your budget below.

Budget item	Month 1	Month 2	Month 3	Month 4...
1) Firstly add in your income:				
Salary	X	X	X	X
Investment income	X	X	X	X
Other income	X	X	X	X
2) Next deduct the items which will contribute to your wealth first, e.g.				
Emergency fund	(X)	(X)	(X)	(X)
Debt repayment	(X)	(X)	(X)	(X)
3) Deduct your essential living expenses next, such as:				
Mortgage	(X)	(X)	(X)	(X)
Utilities	(X)	(X)	(X)	(X)
Travel	(X)	(X)	(X)	(X)
Food	(X)	(X)	(X)	(X)
Insurance	(X)	(X)	(X)	(X)
4) Finally, whatever is left over is discretionary spend:				
Meals out	(X)	(X)	(X)	(X)
TV subscriptions	(X)	(X)	(X)	(X)
Clothes	(X)	(X)	(X)	(X)
Pub visits	(X)	(X)	(X)	(X)

Whilst the format your budget takes is up to you, the budget set out in this way means you are prioritising your financial freedom first and spending your money in the order recommended above. I have also laid the budget out like this to help demonstrate the trade-off you have between your budget categories, for example, the less you spend on entertainment and living costs, the more you can funnel towards wealth building activity, helping you to achieve financial freedom sooner.

***

A few practical pointers:

I would suggest writing out your budget in a Microsoft Excel spreadsheet. I have seen some online apps and none really work for me, so I tend to stick to Excel as I can tailor it exactly to my needs (I also then avoid sharing my data with tech companies). If you don't feel comfortable using Excel, a pen and paper is the next best alternative in my opinion. I would suggest drawing out the budget table as outlined above on a landscape A3 piece of paper. Anything is better than nothing and not being computer literate is no excuse not to control your money.

If you get confused by having all of your earnings and spending going through a single bank account, an effective remedy could be to open a bank account for your essential living expenses and another for your discretionary spending - this would stop spending your utility bill money on a few extra pints on a Friday night! A slight alternative to separate bank accounts is to use 'money jars', which involves withdrawing your spending budget in cash and putting it into different jars dedicated to a spend category, for instance, you may have one for rent/utilities (if you can pay in cash), one for grocery shopping, one for travel/fuel, one for entertainment and so on. This has the benefit of you being able to actually see the cash (which is proven to reduce spending versus using credit cards) and you know that when it's gone, it's gone, and you have to stop spending.

I would also recommend having a monthly dedicated 'money day' or 'budget review day' where you go through your bank and credit card statements and compare your *actual* spend to your budget. The difference between the budget and actual spend is your variance, and you need to understand why you either spent more or less than you budgeted. This may seem like a chore, but it will mean that you are 100% on top of your finances and it will not only be really encouraging to monitor your progress towards your objectives but could also have the impact of distilling greater discipline for sticking to your budget during the following month and beyond.

There is a reason why big businesses use budgets to control spend, achieve their revenue targets, and ensure investors get their expected return. Budgets are the lifeblood of businesses and should therefore be the same for your personal finances. Throughout my career I have prepared numerous complicated budgets, for everything from selling mobile phones, to producing football matches, to buying broadband routers, and I have applied the same budgeting methods and techniques to my own finances and have found them invaluable in my financial freedom journey.

Summary:

A budget is key to controlling your finances and achieving your financial freedom. There is no right or wrong way to budget and it may take a few attempts to find something that works for you, the important thing is that you are doing it. Setting your objectives, defining your goals, and building your initial budget will be time consuming and I recommend setting aside at least 8 hours for it, but I guarantee it will be time well spent and will give you the direction and purpose you need in your financial life. As you start populating your budget, it will only be a matter of time before you start reallocating money from your discretionary spend to wealth building activity!

It is important to allocate time each month to review and evaluate progress against your budget. Although this may seem like a chore, it is so important to ensure you remain on track to achieving your objectives. In no time, you will be able to review your actual spending and saving in a heartbeat and it may even become something you start looking forward to (I know I do); there is something motivating knowing you are making progress towards your financial dreams.

Right then, the best advice now is to just keep calm and start budgeting!

Part Three: Financial Freedom Framework

The Framework for your financial freedom

This section of the book takes the financial concepts and theories covered in the previous chapters and combines them into my Financial Freedom Framework, hereafter referred to as the 'Framework'. The Framework is intended to leave you with zero consumer debt, a fully paid for house, and investments which will provide you with sufficient income to sustain your desired lifestyle indefinitely.

The Framework is designed to act as your roadmap, an easy to follow step by step guide you can follow at any stage of your life, to achieve your freedom. There are seven steps in total and although, ideally, they should be completed sequentially, there is flexibility, especially when it comes to repaying your mortgage and investing. The Framework is split into two key phases: the first being to understand your situation before paying off consumer debts, maximising pension contributions, and building up an emergency fund; and the second being focusing your efforts on aggressively investing and or overpaying your mortgage. Each phase is underpinned by continuous learning and development, protecting yourself through insurance, and continuous evaluation of your objectives and financial position.

* * *

As you will now be aware, the key to achieving financial freedom is simple: maximise your wealth building fund by minimising your expenses, maximising your income and directing such income towards the wealth building activity that is appropriate at the relevant step of your journey (as demonstrated in the Framework).

In addition to the Framework, I have developed a Financial Freedom Formula, hereafter referred to as the 'Formula', which outlines the maths behind this approach. When I was learning about financial freedom, I found I had to continually refer to a number of different resources to get a thorough understanding of the various concepts and steps involved. The aim of the Framework and Formula is to provide a combination of tools that work together to provide you with everything you need to know about achieving your financial freedom in a simple and easy to use guide.

Throughout the remaining chapters, I will explain each of the Framework steps in more detail before demonstrating how the Framework can be applied with some realistic scenarios located in the appendix.

* * *

Financial Freedom (It's Easy When You Know How)

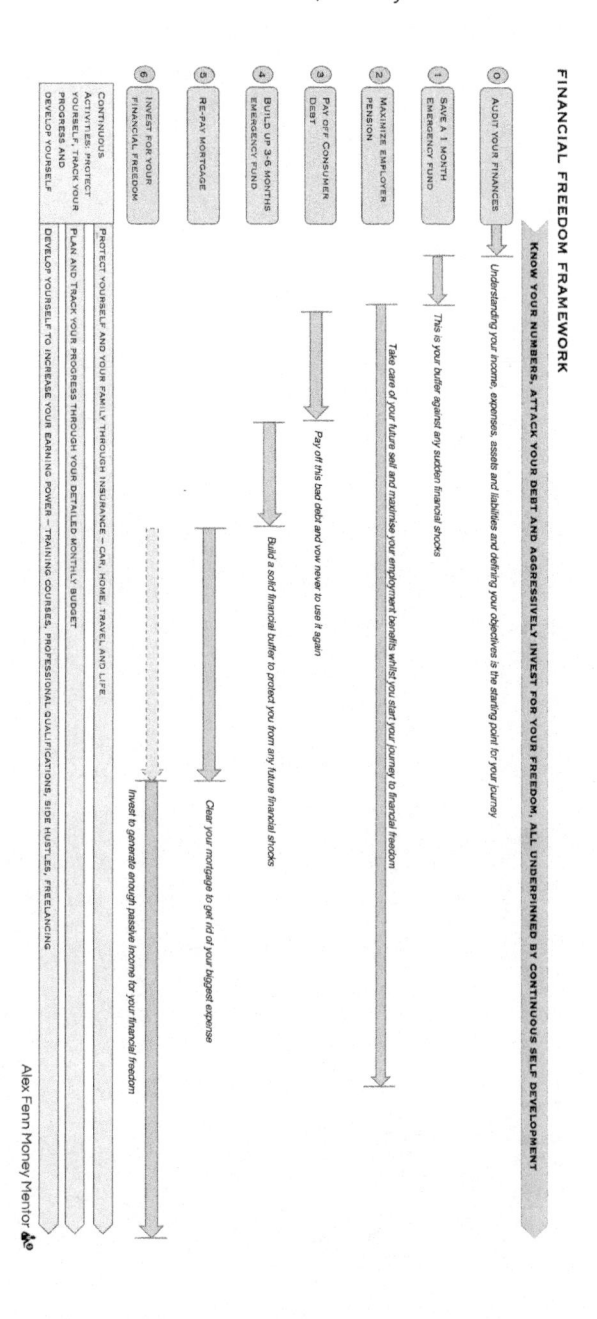

FINANCIAL FREEDOM FRAMEWORK

KNOW YOUR NUMBERS, ATTACK YOUR DEBT AND AGGRESSIVELY INVEST FOR YOUR FREEDOM, ALL UNDERPINNED BY CONTINUOUS SELF DEVELOPMENT

- **0. AUDIT YOUR FINANCES** — Understanding your income, expenses, assets and liabilities and defining your objectives is the starting point for your journey
- **1. SAVE A 1 MONTH EMERGENCY FUND** — This is your buffer against any sudden financial shocks
- **2. MAXIMIZE EMPLOYER PENSION** — Take care of your future self and maximise your employment benefits whilst you start your journey to financial freedom
- **3. PAY OFF CONSUMER DEBT** — Pay off this bad debt and vow never to use it again
- **4. BUILD UP 3-6 MONTHS EMERGENCY FUND** — Build a solid financial buffer to protect you from any future financial shocks
- **5. RE-PAY MORTGAGE** — Clear your mortgage to get rid of your biggest expense
- **6. INVEST FOR YOUR FINANCIAL FREEDOM** — Invest to generate enough passive income for your financial freedom

CONTINUOUS ACTIVITIES:
- PROTECT YOURSELF, TRACK YOUR PROGRESS AND DEVELOP YOURSELF
- PROTECT YOURSELF AND YOUR FAMILY THROUGH INSURANCE – CAR, HOME, TRAVEL, AND LIFE
- PLAN AND TRACK YOUR PROGRESS THROUGH YOUR DETAILED MONTHLY BUDGET
- DEVELOP YOURSELF TO INCREASE YOUR EARNING POWER – TRAINING COURSES, PROFESSIONAL QUALIFICATIONS, SIDE HUSTLES, FREELANCING

Alex Fenn Money Mentor

THE FINANCIAL FREEDOM FORMULA

YOUR MAXIMUM INCOME

Maximise your income from diverse sources:
- 9-5 job
- Bonuses
- Overtime
- Commission
- Side hustles
- Royalties
- Dividends
- Rent
- Interest
- Continuous professional development and life long learning

YOUR MINIMUM EXPENSES

Minimise your living expenses:
- Rent / mortgage
- Groceries
- Utilities
- Travel
- Car
- Entertainment
- Clothing
- Insurance

YOUR MAXIMUM WEALTH BUILDING FUND

Continually review your expenses and develop new sources of income to maximise your Wealth Building Fund

CHANNELED TOWARDS

WEALTH BUILDING ACTIVITY

Use your Wealth Building Fund to follow the Financial Freedom Framework steps:
- Build up an emergency fund to cover 1-6 months worth of expenses
- Pay off consumer debt
- Overpay your mortgage
- Invest in assets to build passive income

LEADS TO

FINANCIAL FREEDOM!

Keep following the Financial Freedom Framework until your investments provide enough passive income to cover your expenses, not needing to rely on an employer for income and allowing you to live the life you deserve

Alex Fenn Money Mentor

The financial freedom mindset

Achieving financial freedom is not just about following a framework and set of rules. More importantly, it involves a change to your mindset and the way you think about your time and money. Having the right mindset will pave the way for you to vastly change your financial situation and this chapter, as a prelude to the Steps of the Framework, will explore some common misconceptions and challenge your thinking when it comes to money.

I'd rather have a million dollars than look a million dollars!
Based on the rose-tinted view of the world often cast by advertising and social media, it is easy to associate the millionaire lifestyle with mansions, sports cars, designer clothes and diamond encrusted watches. On the contrary, genuine financial success and freedom doesn't typically manifest itself in this way and is often far more subtle. People who have really made it, likely got to where they are by spending many years driving second hand cars, living in modest houses, and buying clothes from high street brands, as well as saving aggressively, investing in assets and allowing compound interest to work its magic. This can seem quite dull and boring at first, but is an easier pill to swallow when you accept that (i) reality is not always as it seems, and

(ii) by sacrificing *looking* like a million dollars in favour of living below your means you can give yourself the chance of actually *having* a million dollars. Changing your mindset in this way is a key step towards having the substance to live life on your terms.

Nobody gets rich quickly:

Look online and there is an endless stream of investment schemes and day trading, often completely 'risk free', which promise to double or triple your money in a short timeframe - sounds great right?

I hate to be the bearer of bad news, but these are more than likely scams and should be avoided at all costs. Admittedly, there are examples of people becoming wealthy overnight, for example through winning the lottery or inheriting money, but this is not the norm and you shouldn't gamble your financial success on this. In fact, the average millionaire doesn't reach 'millionaire' status until they are in their 50s.[1]

Becoming financially free involves accumulating a significant amount of wealth and involves hard work, discipline, and time. Hear about the entrepreneur that just sold their company for millions of pounds? This is the result of years and years of hard work, grit, determination, and endless sacrifice which is required in order to build up a successful company. When you see the headline, *'XXX sells their company for £Xm'*, remember, this is a culmination of years of effort and definitely did not happen overnight.

Today we live in a society which is 'always on'; a society where it feels that we are always in a rush to achieve and quickly move on to the next step, the next best thing; and a society where everything is all now, now, now! It is important to ensure that this impatience doesn't creep into your financial freedom mindset; financial freedom is a marathon, not a sprint, and it will take years to achieve. You need to remember this and stick to your plan; you will get there with persistence and discipline, and it becomes easier the closer you get.

Don't try to keep up with the Joneses:

Speaking from my own experience of embarking on my financial freedom journey, your behaviour, opinions, and choices vis-à-vis money will often be the complete opposite of many of your friends. You should expect the occasional raised eyebrow and curious conversation. It is therefore vital to remember the 'why?' to your journey when you receive different reactions to the notion of your goals; you are doing this for you and no-one else.

As you progress through your career and your earnings increase, it is normal for your expenses to also increase; you will, at the very least, be tempted to buy more expensive brands, live in more expensive places, drive more expensive cars, go to more expensive restaurants, and holiday in further flung and more luxurious destinations. These traits are all symptoms of lifestyle creep which, as your friends will likely be doing the same, is pretty much hidden in plain sight. Lifestyle creep can also put pressure on you to keep up, even if you don't really want to. Your path to financial freedom requires you to prioritise repaying debts and investing, as opposed to buying the latest technology and designer goods and eating in the most fashionable restaurants. It is inevitable that you will battle against lifestyle creep and it is an important battle to fight and win. Don't try to keep up with the Joneses; it is a never ending battle that you won't win and it can postpone your financial freedom indefinitely.

***

Here is an example to help put this into context. I drive a great car. It is nearly 8 years old and wasn't bought new. It is well looked after and a great run around, but what it isn't is a car that society expects someone with my level of income to drive; as a finance professional, I should be driving a fancy German saloon (if I interpret the adverts correctly!). The fact is, I am keeping the car until it can no longer move, at which point I will replace it with another very practical, used car which I will then also run until it bites the dust. I have no issues with what people think about me when I drive past them or pull up outside their house. I choose not to let other people's purchases or perceptions dictate my behaviour; my Wealth Building Fund is instead working for me in the financial markets, helping me on the way to financial freedom.

When you are at the point of not caring about whether you have the latest smartphone or newest numberplate on your car, it is a great sign that you have the right mindset for achieving financial freedom. I'm not saying temptation will cease; there are always fancy products accompanied by impressive advertisements trying to convince us to buy them, but just remember your long term plan and goal of financial freedom and I am sure the temptation will subside. Shifting your mindset to stop caring too much about what other people think about you based on the material possessions you own is truly liberating and crucial in your quest to becoming financially free.

The true cost of your purchases:

Understanding the true cost of your purchases is really important in helping you achieve your financial freedom, as it will also help you resist when faced with consumerist temptation; consider the following example.

You see the latest £1,000 smartphone and, in the knowledge that your peers are all going to upgrade and in fear of feeling inferior, you decide to buy one. You rationalise the purchase by telling yourself that you work hard for your money, have the money to spend, and, ultimately, it's only £1,000. However, assuming you already have a perfectly workable phone and don't actually *need* a new one, the true cost of the phone is not £1,000. This is because, as an alternative to buying the phone, you have the option to invest this £1,000 in a diversified index fund earning, say, a 6% annual return, meaning your £1,000 would be worth £1,338 in 5 years, £1,790 in 10 years, and £3,207 in 20 years. You are essentially foregoing future investment return by buying something now which is unnecessary and won't actually make a difference to your lifestyle. You may look at this and think, well I don't mind foregoing £3,000 of future returns in order to buy the smartphone today, you may even try to justify it to yourself as being a bit of a 'treat', but this is just one example of many similar purchases you will find yourself making if you don't exercise discipline in your decision making. Buying the latest car, tablet, TV, coffee machine, etc. year after year, quickly adds up and, before you know it, you could be foregoing hundreds of thousands of pounds.

This concept is known as 'opportunity cost' in economics and for every purchase I encourage you to ask yourself, *'what else could I do with this money?'* to help you evaluate the decision from more angles than just simply, *'do I want it and is everyone else going to have it?'*. The ideal scenario is that you ask yourself this question *before* making a purchase but, fear not, it isn't necessarily game over if you make a spontaneous purchase that you haven't fully thought through (subject to the retailer's returns policy, of course!). My partner is an avid online shopper and has devised a strategy for reducing the number of items she keeps, fondly known as 'cash or keep'. Simply, for each item purchased, she asks herself, *'cash or keep?'*, i.e. if the physical amount of money the item cost was next to the item, and she could keep either the money or the item, which would she choose? Going through this extra step enables you to rationally assess the true value of your purchases and undo any unnecessary impulse buys.

Think twice and be mindful about your purchases; only buy what you need; resist temptation; and give yourself the best chance of achieving your freedom.

You don't need to spend a lot to be happy – 'rightsize' your monthly expenses:

I'd like you to think about your happiest times in the last 10-20 years; did these involve spending lots of money? Were you happier eating in that Michelin starred restaurant, or having a picnic on the beach with your family? Were you happier in your, temporarily, brand new car, or your first car (that was perhaps handed down to you by your parents or that you saved your weekend job money to buy)?

Don't get me wrong, I am not against spending money on things that make you happy and truly add value to your life, quite the contrary; you *should* invest in the things that add maximum value. What I am against is the belief that spending more money makes you happier. If you truly evaluate what you really need and want to spend your money on, it could mean that you reach financial freedom earlier than you initially thought. For example, if you decide that you get as much happiness and value from buying your groceries from a budget supermarket as you do a premium one, you could switch to the budget supermarket and increase your Wealth Building Fund by hundreds of pounds per month, with little impact on your lifestyle.

This may require you to readjust your mindset and get into the habit of evaluating your expenses in terms of the happiness and value they give you. Your monthly expenses should be enough to enable you to live in a way that is fulfilling but without any excess and this is important as trimming the excess means (i) you need less money in your financial freedom fund, (ii) your emergency fund lasts longer, and (iii) ultimately, you don't have to rely on your employer for income for as long. Remember, for every £1 you spend, you need to have at least £25 in your investment portfolio in order to support it, so start ridding your life of any expenses which truly don't add value!

Small amounts add up!

You may not believe it, but little things do add up. £5, £10, £15 here and there may not sound like a lot, but small decisions multiplied up and compounded make a huge difference. For instance, saving £15 per week by taking a coffee from home in a travel mug rather than buying a takeaway coffee results in a saving of £60 per month (£720 per year) and is likely to have little impact on your lifestyle. To help break the cycle, ask yourself, 'what is the marginal benefit I receive from having a takeaway coffee versus bringing my own from home?'.

This may seem a bit petty and trivial, but the long term financial impact of saving these small sums can be huge. You also work hard for your money and it should not be let go of so easily. Let's consider another example. Let's assume you spend £5 per day on lunch whilst at work. If you were to instead make your own lunch, at a cost of £1, you would save £4 per day (that's £20 per week). Assuming you work 40 weeks per year, that's a saving of £800 per year and, if you were to work for 20 years and invested this £800 for those 20 years, you would have just under £30,000! All from something as simple as taking your own lunch to work.

Everything has value:

Just because you no longer want a certain item, it doesn't mean it is not worth something to someone else. As part of a periodical cleanse of your possessions, you should look to sell anything you no longer need and put the money towards your wealth building activities. There are hundreds of websites offering a platform to sell almost anything from designer clothes to antiques, not to mention the traditional outlets of local car boot sales and even pawn shops to help convert your unwanted possessions into cash. If you struggle to make a decision about whether to keep something, you can apply the *'six/six'* rule which means if you haven't used anything in the last six months and won't use it in the next 6 months, sell it, or if it doesn't have a monetary value, donate it.

Even though it may be difficult at first, as we tend to attach emotions to possessions, once you get over this initial bump and remember that memories exist within us and not items, it becomes rather enjoyable! There is also a secondary benefit to you psychologically by decluttering. Because clutter takes up headspace and causes stress, getting rid of all of your excess 'stuff' will de-stress you and put you in the right frame of mind to tackle your finances, as they say, 'a tidy house means a tidy mind'. I personally found this when I downsized my wardrobe, sold my unwanted books and DVDs and donated a bunch of other stuff; my stress levels reduced instantly and I felt a true sense of contentment, I can't recommend it highly enough.

An alternative to selling your possessions and buying new, is to 'up-cycle'; could you re-paint that old cabinet or alter your clothes by adding sequins, for instance? If you find yourself with a hidden talent for up-cycling, it could also become a side business where you buy and renovate unwanted items and sell them at a profit. For a good few years, my partner and I wanted a new kitchen and were saving up for a modern re-build which we expected to cost upwards of £15,000. However, our up-cycling mentality (combined with a fair amount of patience) saw us re-paint the existing kitchen cabinets and tiles, polish up the flooring and worktops, and replace only our appliances for more modern ones. The result? A 'new' kitchen and a saving of at least £12,000!

On the flip side, if you are looking to *buy* something, don't just default to buying brand new. It is good practice to check second hand websites such as Gumtree or Facebook Marketplace, or even charity shops, which now sell a huge variety of quality clothes, books, and gifts (sometimes even those that haven't been worn/used). Just adding in this step to your purchasing decisions could mean you save thousands over your lifetime and is a habit you should adopt; you will be amazed at the discounts available by shopping around – it will contribute towards offsetting your carbon footprint too!

Stop looking at the price, start calculating the time and impact on your freedom:

As well as thinking of the price of something in terms of opportunity cost, i.e. *'what could this money be worth if I invested it?'*, think of it in terms of how much time you would need to spend at work in order to earn the money to pay for it. In order to do this, you need to know how much your *true* hourly wage is. This is not just simply your earnings divided by your contracted hours, but the time (and money!) spent commuting, decompressing after work, buying work clothes, and doing anything else you wouldn't otherwise have to if you didn't have to work for your employer. Vicki Robin's book, 'Your Money or Your Life', provides readers with a very useful step by step guide to calculating their *true* hourly wage. Word of caution: it is unbelievable how much lower one's true hourly wage is, than you would think...

To get started, I would suggest converting every purchase into an 'hours at work equivalent'. For example, if some tempting new product costs £250 and you earn £10 per hour, you would have to work 25 hours, more than three days, in order to buy it. Ask yourself, is the item worth the sacrifice? Would the happiness you gain from it be worth the 25 hours spent at work? This works on both a large and small scale, so can be applied in the same way to your £5 artisan coffee.

I personally find that this method helps me to make a rounded decision about every purchase and, if I decide to make such purchase, I appreciate it much more than I otherwise would. It also has the effect of making me view my purchases as long term and looking after things so they last as long as possible to avoid being in the position of trading more of my time to be able to buy replacements, thereby unnecessarily pushing out my financial freedom date.

Prioritise getting out of debt, it is not good!

We are in a society which seems to be very comfortable with carrying debt; debt has been normalised and is just seen as part of being an adult. Rewind to the 1950s and if you wanted to buy an expensive item such as a car or a holiday, you had to save up and pay cash or go to your bank manager who would only lend you money if you could guarantee repayment. If you couldn't afford it or convince your bank manager, you went without. Fast forward to the 2020s and it is almost unheard of for people not to have some or all of credit cards, hire purchase, car leases, bank loans, pay day loans and store cards. We are using debt to fund a lifestyle we can't afford!

A key takeaway from this book is that debt is not good for you and as long as you have debt you will not have financial freedom. If you do have debt, you need to be of the mindset that it is like having creepy crawlies all over you; it is something to get rid of as soon as you possibly can and, once debt free, promise yourself not to get into debt again.

Become a (sort of) minimalist:

Okay, you don't need to convert to minimalism to achieve financial freedom, but the mentality of minimalists is admirable and, even though you don't need to go to this extreme, adopting some of their traits is advisable. Minimalists live on the bare minimum required for their existence and it applies to every area of their life, from the size of their house to the number of spoons they have. Hear me out. As minimalists put so much thought into each purchase, it makes it easier to appreciate each purchase with no regrets or guilt. I strongly advise that you research two very inspirational people, Joshua Fields Milburn and Ryan Nicodemus, otherwise known as 'The Minimalists', who left six figure corporate careers, large houses, multiple cars and designer wardrobes to live a life without excess and they, by their own admission, have never been happier.

* * *

Reducing the excess in your life will have a huge impact on your bank account, as you will no longer sacrifice your hard earned money for that same dress in a different colour, the latest model of coffee machine or that new subscription which delivers pre-prepared food to your door. In addition to saving you money, the impact this lifestyle will have on your mental health is immeasurable. Having an abundance of items, subscriptions, and accounts comes with the immense pressure of having to maintain them. Freeing yourself of surplus does wonders for your mind, removing the unnecessary noise and creating a sense of peace.

I am not a full minimalist (yet), but I do subscribe to the Scandinavian concept known as 'Lagom' which translates as *'not too much, not too little, just the right amount'*. Lagom is about creating balance in every aspect of your life and being mindful about your existence. Adopting Lagom in my life has had a massive positive impact on both my mental and financial health and I couldn't recommend it enough.

Summary:
The hardest part of achieving financial freedom is not the knowing how but adopting the right mindset. Fundamentally, it requires you to stop prioritising how you are perceived by others; success can manifest itself in various ways and it's up to you whether you demonstrate your success through the volume of expensive material possessions you have or by achieving financial freedom. Changing your thinking when it comes to purchases will mean you make truly well rounded decisions, only buying things you need and really appreciating what you buy. The aim is to avoid mindlessly buying random things just because the adverts tell you to. Making small changes and consistently applying them for a long time will have amazing

impacts on your financial situation and is key to achieving your freedom.

Key takeaways:
- Financial freedom is not about looking richer than you are but being richer than you look; you need to care less about what other people might think – you do you. You are running your own race which may be at odds to most of those around you, so keep calm and stay the course.
- You should evaluate purchases in terms of the opportunity cost (i.e. what else could I do with my money?) and how much time it will take you to earn the purchase price of the item, this will ensure you make the right purchase decision.
- When you do decide to buy, be mindful of your purchases, look after and appreciate the things you own.
- We are in a society which normalises credit cards, buy now pay later, mortgages and pay day loans; get rid of your debt to give yourself the best chance of becoming financially free.
- Don't always buy things brand new, look to up-cycle where possible and explore the second hand market - you will be amazed at the discounts available from shopping around.
- Regularly evaluate your possessions and sell anything you don't need, directing the proceeds towards wealth building activity.
- Embrace minimalism or 'Lagom' and reduce the amount of clutter in every aspect of your life to improve both your mental and financial health.

Framework Step 0 - audit your finances

Step 0 - before you do anything - do a financial audit:

Before you start your journey to financial freedom, you need to understand where your money comes from, where it goes, what you own and what you owe. This is done by undertaking an audit of your finances which will become the foundation of your financial plan. Even though an audit may sound onerous and boring, I cannot emphasise enough how important this is and, without it, I'd even argue you can never become financially free. This chapter will give you a step by step guide on how to conduct your financial audit and explain how this feeds into your financial freedom.

As a word of warning, confronting your financial position can be a bit scary, not just because it's possible you have accounts all over the place for which you have maybe forgotten a password or two, but mainly because of what the audit is going to tell you; all of your financial decisions, both good and bad, and everything in between, will be laid bare. To combat this apprehension, the only comfort I can offer you is to say that the more you understand your situation, the less intimidated you will be and the easier it is to tackle it head on. It is likely that you will find the process to be therapeutic and cathartic, boosting not only your confidence, but also taking a huge weight off your shoulders.

There are three key elements to the audit: firstly, calculating your average income and expenses, secondly, understanding your assets and your liabilities, and then combining these into the third element, your net worth.

As it will involve quite a bit of data entry from various sources, the best way to undertake your audit is in a Microsoft Excel spreadsheet. I would suggest having one tab for your income and expenses and another for your assets and liabilities. If you are not comfortable with Excel though, this can still be done with a pen and paper or via one of the many Apps and online tools available to help consolidate your financials. I have tried a number of Apps but continue to return to Excel as it can be easily tailored to any financial situation.

Step 0.1 – calculate your average income and expenses:

This can be the scary bit as it involves looking back over the last six months of your bank and credit card statements and writing down all of your income and expenses, capturing what you have earned, spent, saved and invested. The aim of this activity is to understand your average monthly income, essential expenses (i.e. mortgage/rent/utilities), discretionary spend (i.e. entertainment/meals out/clothes), savings, investments and debt payments and thus identify the *true* cost of your lifestyle and what your starting Wealth Building Fund is.

The best way to do this is to download or print all of your bank and credit card statements from the last six months and transpose them into the 'income and expenses' tab of your spreadsheet. For each transaction, I would suggest writing down the detail and assigning it a high level category, for example, if you have a basic salary and overtime, the high level category for these transactions could be 'Income'. The reason for assigning a high level category, is that it makes analysing your finances much easier and helps you compartmentalise your spending and income, which then makes budgeting simpler.

Your spreadsheet for income and expenses could look like this:

Income / Expense	High level category	Transaction detail	Month	Amount
Expense	Groceries	Weekly food shop	Jan	£75
Expense	Housing	Mortgage payment	Jan	£800
Expense	Travel	Train ticket	Jan	£100
Income	Salary	Employer pay	Jan	£1,700
Etc.	Etc.	Etc.	Etc.	Etc.

A simple table like this will take a few hours to complete but it is one of the best investments you will make.

Once you have captured all of your data in this format, you need to summarise it into an easy to understand picture of your finances. A good way to do this is in a pivot table. To create a pivot table:
- highlight your data
- click the 'insert' button in the top ribbon
- select 'pivot table'
- add your month to the column section, and then high level category to the row, followed by the amount in the value section

The name of each of your categories is up to you and comes down to individual preference, but there are general buckets which I tend to use with clients, as follows: income, housing, groceries, savings, investments, debt payments, car payments, insurance, utilities/phone/internet, groceries, healthcare, leisure and discretionary. The key is to have enough categories that are mutually exclusive and encapsulate all of your information without having too many that it becomes cumbersome and unusable.

Now to calculate your average income and expenses. This is done by dividing each of your total income and expenses by the number of months covered. If you had large one-off expenses in your analysis which are not recurring, such as having to pay to fix your car, deduct this from your expenses before you calculate the average so as not to over-inflate your averages. To gauge the success of this exercise, you should be able to recall your average spend for each category by heart and, most importantly, know the value of your 'Wealth Building Fund'.

You should be really pleased with yourself for getting this far, everything from this point is less manual and much quicker. Now you know your numbers, I suggest reviewing your detailed spending by looking in detail at each category, evaluating the value each transaction gives you. For example, within discretionary, if you spend £100 on average each month going to the pub, is it worth it, or would you have had as good a time inviting your friends round to your house and spending £25 on some supermarket beers? Similarly, would you get as much (or more) satisfaction and happiness by cooking a meal for your friends for half the price of eating out a restaurant? These are the kinds of questions you should be asking yourself for all of your expenses.

The importance of carrying out this review of your transactions to determine the value and happiness each transaction brings, should not be underestimated; repointing just small amounts of money to your WBF can have an incredible impact on your future financial position. Following such review, the money you save through eliminating the expenses you no longer need, effectively means you are giving yourself a free pay rise and this is a great feeling. In addition, simply knowing you are spending the minimum amount you need to live happily and with no excess is likely to bring a real sense of contentment.

Step 0.2 - list out your assets:

Now you have analysed and evaluated your monthly income and expenses, it is time to calculate your net worth - that is your assets minus your liabilities. As mentioned above, I would recommend capturing this in a separate 'assets and liabilities' tab in your spreadsheet, starting with your assets. Again, it is recommended that you apply a similar high level categorisation system that you applied to your income and expenses. The categories I use for clients for this activity tend to fall into the following buckets: pension, investment portfolio, emergency fund, other cash savings, house equity, cars, jewellery and house contents. Again, this isn't a prescriptive list, and you can use appropriate ones for your situation as long as they encapsulate all of your assets.

In terms of what should be considered 'assets', I tend to apply a valuation threshold of £100 for individual items. In theory, your knives and forks are assets but, as you would be unlikely to get any meaningful amount of money for these if you decided to sell them, I would leave them out of your calculations. That said, an antique bone china serving plate worth £150 should definitely be listed as one of your assets, so an element of discretion should be exercised.

Ideally, once you have determined which items should

appear in your list of assets, you would assign a value to each item in a long list, but, to make the exercise less time consuming, you can group certain items into one entry. For instance, your beds, furniture, TV, table and chairs etc. can be collated and described as 'house contents'. Unless you have had your assets formally valued, it can be difficult to attach a value to them for the purposes of this exercise. You should use the best available valuation estimate for each of your assets – this will be more easily determined for some assets (such as your pension and investments) but, for others, it is best to err on the side of caution and use a prudent estimate.

Once you have a complete list of your assets, the sum of the value of all items on such list is the *value of your assets*. As this is a snapshot of your assets at a particular point in time, the individual valuations should be reviewed at least annually, or whenever there is a significant change to your situation, e.g. if you receive a windfall cash bonus or buy a new car for cash.

Step 0.3 - list out your liabilities:

This step involves listing out all of the money that you owe and includes your mortgage, credit cards, car leases, consumer credit and any other item that requires you to make repayments. To clarify, this does not include your utility bills, grocery shopping or rent (these are all expenses, not liabilities). It is important you note down as much information as possible about each liability, for example, instead of just writing down that you have £1,000 of credit card debt, note down the interest rate, minimum payments, any offers (e.g. six months interest free on purchases) and the date on which any offers expire. The reason for noting down all of these details is to not only get your house in order and know all the information about your liabilities, the information also feeds heavily into your financial planning activity.

The sum of this list represents the total amount you owe and, as with your assets, you should review this at least annually or when a significant change has happened.

Step 0.4 - combine your analysis:

The final thing you need to do is to combine all of your hard work into a simple summary of your financial position. Firstly, calculate your net worth by deducting your liabilities from your assets. For example, if you have £100,000 of assets and £60,000 of liabilities, your net worth would be £40,000 (£100,000 - £60,000).

Secondly, you need to summarise your average income and expenses, having adjusted each of these to reflect any reductions to your spending and repointing to your wealth building fund. For example, if you felt you were unhappy spending an average of £100 on meals out per month and, consequently, committed to only spending £50 going forward, the £50 saving should be put towards your WBF and be reflected accordingly in your final income and expense breakdown.

Summary:

Once you have finished this step, give yourself a pat on the back. You will at this point be fully equipped to plan your financial future because you will know exactly where your money comes from and where it goes, have maximised your wealth building fund, and know your net worth.

Hopefully undertaking this exercise also illustrates the 'game of money' to you and how your categories of finance interact with each other; repointing money towards wealth building activity and increasing your WBF to reduce debt and/or increase investments leads to an increase in your net worth which impacts the timing of your financial freedom.

Ultimately, undertaking a financial audit is fundamental to achieving financial freedom. Without understanding your financial position, you can't proceed with the rest of your journey. I won't kid you; it is time consuming and can be quite intimidating as it involves confronting your past financial decisions, both the good and the bad. However, the benefits are extraordinary, not just because it puts you on the path to financial success but also because of the calming psychological impact of knowing you have your affairs in order – this is the feeling that is hard to describe and best experienced first-hand. So, what are you waiting for?

Framework Step 1 - save one month's expenses in an emergency fund

You may have heard the term, *'save for a rainy day'*. This is a fundamental concept in finance and one which I believe has been hardwired into our evolution from the animal kingdom as a response to uncertain times; just think of a squirrel burying nuts for the winter. An emergency fund is your financial equivalent of a squirrel burying its nuts for winter, as it acts as a pot of money which is there for you to use during the harder times in life, be that due to a job loss, a car breakdown, your boiler packing in, or something else unexpected.

It is important to mention that an emergency fund is not there to fund the difference between an economy and business class flight or an extra few days stay in a hotel, it should be seen as an insurance policy to cover the essentials in times of need. An emergency fund provides you with a cushion against life's unexpected surprises and acts as a barrier against you having to go into debt or being forced to sell your investments in order to fund the cost of any such shocks.

In the UK, the financial situation in which we find ourselves when it comes to savings is unbelievable; one in three people don't have any savings at all and 41% don't have enough money to last them until their next pay check[1]. In other words, almost three quarters (!!!) of adults in the UK can't survive for longer than a month without relying on a salary from their employer. The story is similar in the USA whereby it was found that almost 40% of people were unable to meet an unexpected $1,000 expense.[2] How can these be the statistics for some of the richest countries in the world?! As a result of living on such a financial cliff edge, people commonly rely on credit cards, pay day loans and other short term borrowings to cover the cost of an emergency expense. This behaviour creates a vicious circle because following the emergency expenditure, the time spent repaying expensive credit card debt not only creates more stress but it reverses any prior progress towards building wealth. For many people, this unfortunate circle epitomises their financial life indefinitely. Take action - don't fall victim to this trap.

There is another saying, *'it's only when the tide goes out that you find out who isn't wearing any swimming trunks'*. This also applies quite nicely to personal finances. In other words, only when you stop earning money do you realise how much of a precarious situation you are in. Bearing this in mind, you soon realise that having true financial stability is worth more than appearing well off but lacking in substance.

In order to avoid financial entrapment and create true financial stability, traditional financial planning suggests you should aim to have between three and six months of your expenses saved in an easily accessible account if you are working, and at least 12 months of expenses saved if you are retired. This may seem like a lot but, once you have this financial barrier in place, hopefully you won't have to touch it and it will act as a permanent financial cushion, removing a lot of stress from your life. In addition, having an easily accessible buffer avoids forcing you to sell any investments in order to fund an emergency (which could lead you to selling investments at a loss thereby undoing all your good work).

So how do you go about building this financial barrier? The first step is to save an amount equal to one month of your essential expenses in an instant access savings account or even a separate current account dedicated to your emergency fund. What constitutes 'essential expenses' is often a point for debate, but the way I see it is that these are the costs you would have no choice but to pay if you were to be sacked from your job tomorrow, for example:

- mortgage or rent
- utilities (gas, electricity, internet, phone)
- council tax
- debt / credit card / car repayments
- childcare
- essential travel
- very basic groceries

You will notice that this list does not include entertainment, takeaways, nights out, new clothes or premium groceries. Put frankly, if you are in a situation where you have no income, you should not be spending money on anything that is not absolutely essential for your survival.

As you'll likely have gathered, the lower the essential or 'fixed' cost of your lifestyle, the less money you need in your emergency fund or, looking at it another way, the longer you could last without income. Ring fencing an emergency fund is the first step in your long journey to financial freedom and will give you the peace of mind that you could cope with a financial emergency without having to reach for the credit card or loans, putting yourself into financial difficulty. This peace of mind is worth its weight in gold and puts you ahead of the majority of people in the UK so will likely also be a huge boost to your confidence.

Once in place, you need to resist the temptation of spending your emergency fund on anything other than emergency expenses. If you are not used to having savings, this can be difficult but remind yourself of the effort and sacrifices you made to put yourself in this preferable position and remember that you would only be stealing from your future self if you gave into this temptation.

Ways to build up your emergency fund:
It is really important to build and maximise your one month emergency fund as quickly as possible and there are several options available to help you to achieve this. Firstly, remember those surplus items we considered earlier which we decided would be more valuable to someone else than to ourselves and consequently sold? Well, the proceeds from selling those unwanted possessions can give you a great head start to building up your emergency fund. Secondly, allocate your full Wealth Building Fund to your emergency fund until it equals one month of your expenses.

Where do I save it?
It is important that your emergency fund can be accessed as soon as it is required and therefore an 'instant access savings account' is your best option. These accounts pay very little interest (below 1% is the norm) but this money is there to protect you in the event of an emergency, not to make you wealthy. With this in mind, another option is to house your emergency fund in a standalone current account, isolated

from the account housing your disposable cash. Whilst, theoretically, you could have your emergency fund saved as hard cash, I would advise against this for several reasons: it can be lost, it doesn't earn *any* interest, and it can be all too tempting to grab the cash and go to the pub on a whim. Although the aim of your emergency fund is not to generate you interest income, I would still recommend reviewing the interest on the instant access savings/current accounts available in the market regularly and moving your fund to the account with the best rate. A few basis points of interest is worth it, even when rates are so low, as it means your money is working as hard as possible for you.

Why save money when I have debts to repay?

This is a pertinent question as it can seem illogical to be saving money whilst you have expensive debts to repay, but there is rationale behind this. To be clear, I am not suggesting you build your emergency fund *instead* of repaying the minimum payments on your debts – nothing should trump those. This is more about pointing remaining funds towards building your emergency fund rather than overpaying debts. Let's consider a 'sliding doors' scenario.

Example:

Imagine you are in a good financial position and have decided to take out a credit card for house renovations, which has an offer rate of 0% interest for 18 months on purchases made within the first three months. You use the credit card to buy decorating supplies and furniture, amounting to £3,600. You took out the credit card to help you with cashflow and knowing you could cover the £200 per month repayment needed for 18 months to avoid incurring interest. Following an audit of your finances in line with Step 0 of the Framework, you realise that rather than the anticipated £200 you have £400 left for wealth building activity. You know that £200 of this is spoken for and mull over what to do with the remaining £200.

Scenario one: you remember reading somewhere that *'debt is bad'* and having debt is *'like having creepy crawlies all over you'*. After a while deliberating, you decide to point all £400 towards clearing the credit card debt, consequently clearing the debt in 9 months, half the anticipated time – marvellous.

Scenario two: whilst you remember reading somewhere that *'debt is bad'* and having debt is *'like having creepy crawlies all over you'*, you also remember reading of the importance of having an emergency fund. With this in mind and, importantly, knowing that you will clear the credit card debt before it incurs any interest through your regular £200 per month repayments, you decide to point the remaining £200 towards your emergency fund each month.

Five months into your credit card term, your car service and MOT fall due. Upon inspection, it is deemed that your car is not roadworthy and requires £650 worth of repairs. You have no choice but to give the immediate go ahead on the repairs as you use your car daily to commute to and from work and you are unable to work from home.

Scenario one continued: you have no emergency fund and no spare money. Next month, you could hold back £200 of the £400 you have spent paying off your credit card for the past five months, but your need for the cash is urgent and £200 wouldn't even cover a third of your bill. You consider your financial situation and determine that the only option available to you is to take out further credit, either by adding the repair costs to your existing credit card (and incurring interest on that amount given that the three month purchase offer window has expired) or via other means. You feel frustrated and anxious, knowing that rather than pointing your hard earned money towards wealth building activity for the next several months, you are going to be paying off that credit plus interest.

Scenario two continued: having paid £200 a month into your emergency fund for 5 months, you realise that you have £1,000 at your disposal for the emergency, unexpected, costs to repair your car. You are left with £350 in your emergency fund and can continue to pay £200 into such fund until you have the recommended amount equal to one month's expenses at your disposal. You write off the experience as an inconvenience and feel gratitude for and proud of yourself for exercising the financial discipline you read about in that book that time...

Whilst this example is fairly binary, it is a helpful illustration as to the benefits of prioritising your emergency fund. By having a cash buffer to cover any emergencies, it prevents you from turning to alternative forms of funding such as pay day loans, credit cards and overdrafts which require yet another monthly payment with interest thereby pushing you further away from financial freedom. More importantly, there is a huge psychological benefit of having such buffer resulting in fewer sleepless nights hoping that your car passes its MOT and your boiler doesn't break down. The comfort you get from knowing you are financially in a safe place if there is an unexpected bill, is indescribable (I speak from personal experience here). The only thing you have to worry about is the inconvenience of sorting out your car repair, boiler replacement, new washing machine, or whatever other random thing that goes wrong, without being overwhelmed with panic about the cost.

This initial emergency fund will be a cornerstone of your financial success, not only providing that emergency cover but also instilling the financial discipline required to live below your means and make tough decisions to sell unwanted items and not buy surplus in order to build up your emergency fund. Exercising this discipline forms a habit; a habit that you will carry with you through the rest of your financial journey.

Although the Framework suggests building up one month's expenses as an initial emergency fund, it is just a guide. If you are unable to reduce the interest rates on your debts (through negotiating and balance transfers), it may be right for you to save a lower initial emergency fund. If you have exceptionally expensive debts to clear, you may be more comfortable with say, £500 in your initial emergency fund before moving to Step 3 to aggressively clear your debts. The decision is ultimately dependent on your situation but it is important that you do have an emergency fund.

What happens if I need to use it?

In the unfortunate event that you need to use your emergency fund, it is important that you build it back up as quickly as possible by diverting cash from your wealth building activity to the emergency fund. For example, if you are paying £300 per month towards your credit card debt for which the minimum payment is £50, and you had to use £1,000 of your emergency fund to repair your car, you would divert £250 to your emergency fund for four months to top it back up, whilst paying the minimum payment towards your credit card.

* * *

Is this the same as my holiday savings?
Absolutely not! Your emergency fund is only there as an insurance policy; the way to look at it is that it doesn't belong to you but to your future self. If you did use the fund to go on holiday, you wouldn't be happy with yourself if in six months' time you couldn't afford to replace your boiler and had to endure cold showers throughout the winter! Save it, leave it there and only use it when you absolutely have to!

If you want to save up for a significant expense such as a holiday, replacement car, or house renovations, you should save money in a separate savings account and only when you have eliminated any high interest debts should you be looking to spend any significant amount of money on non-wealth building activity.

Summary:
'Save for a rainy day', is the longest standing piece of advice when it comes to personal finance and having money set aside for emergencies is the bedrock of financial success. As such, Step 1 of the Framework is to save one month's worth of expenses to cover you for any unexpected events that life can, and often does, throw at you.

Key takeaways:
- Save your emergency fund in an instant access savings or current account, review the interest rates regularly and move your fund to the account with the highest available interest rate.
- Continually review your monthly expenses and reflect any changes in your fund, e.g. if your utility bills rise by £50 per month, then you need to increase your emergency fund by a corresponding amount.

- If you need to dip into your emergency fund, divert money from your wealth building activity to your fund to build it back up to the appropriate level.
- Sell as many of your unwanted items to kick start your emergency fund; it is amazing how much money you have tied up in dormant objects around your house.
- Your emergency fund is not to be used for anything other than unexpected expenses; it is not to be used for holidays or an 'emergency' Friday night takeaway!

Framework Step 2 - maximise your employer pension contributions

Now you have saved one month's worth of expenses in your emergency fund (of which you should be really proud, as it has put you ahead of a lot of people!), the next step of the Framework is to make sure you are taking full advantage of your employer pension scheme by maximising your employer's pension contributions. In the UK, employers can be very generous with their matching contributions so it is important you take full advantage of this; after all, your employer will take all they can from you in the call of duty, so when they are offering you free money, you should bite their hand off! Most employers offer a pension match based on your own contributions, for example, if you contribute 5%, your employer will also contribute 5% for free. It is important to explore your employer pension options, so speak to HR, your manager and other colleagues to understand the offering and ensure you contribute the amount required to take full advantage of the employer match.

I cannot emphasise enough how important it is to contribute to your pension - investing in a pension is often overlooked by people which can lead to having a significantly underfunded retirement. To illustrate, the average pension pot in the UK in 2020 was just over £63,000[1] which, although may sound like a lot, would only give you an annual income of around £2,500, assuming you draw down at a rate of 4%.

The following graph illustrates the stark difference between getting your employer match versus just your own contributions. The graph contains a few assumptions for simplicity, but it really helps demonstrate the impact a small monthly change can have on your retirement income.

The calculations are based on a 25 year old earning £30,000 per year, retiring at 67 years old (giving 42 years of pension contributions), earning an annual return of 5% and then drawing down 4% of their pension per year as income. Admittedly this example is simplistic but it is designed to highlight the importance of maximising your employer pension contributions and demonstrate the impact a small monthly change can have on your retirement income. The columns in the graph represent the annual income you would receive from your pension under various scenarios where you contribute a set percentage per month to your pension both just individually and with your employer matching your contributions.

* * *

Annual retirement income at different monthly contribution levels with and without employer matches

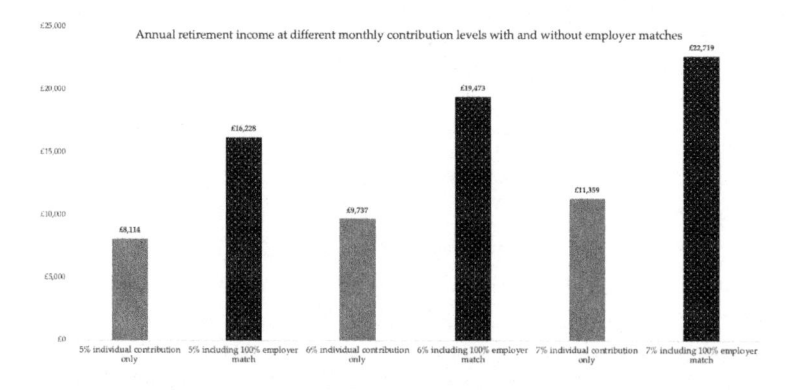

5% individual contribution only	£8,114
5% including 100% employer match	£16,228
6% individual contribution only	£9,737
6% including 100% employer match	£19,473
7% individual contribution only	£11,359
7% including 100% employer match	£22,719

As you can see, if you only contributed 5% of your monthly salary (£125 per month) to your pension from age 25 to 67, you could draw an income of £8,114 per year. However, taking advantage of your employer match would double your retirement income - FOR FREE!! You can also see from the graph the huge impact a small monthly change can have on your retirement; by increasing your monthly contribution from 5% (£125) to 7% (£175), your annual income upon retirement would increase from £16,228 to £22,719. By contributing an additional £50 per month to your pension, instead of spending it in the pub, your annual income in retirement would increase by almost £6,500 or £540 per month (which is 10x your monthly salary sacrifice!!). Employer pension matches do vary by employer, but it is important you take advantage of them to the fullest extent as it can make a gigantic difference to your future.

How this fits in with your financial freedom journey:

As part of Step 1, you saved one month's worth of expenses in your emergency fund to protect you from any unforeseen events avoiding the need to rely on expensive credit cards and loans in emergencies. This Step 2 ensures you are maximising the free money from your employer and getting it to work for you as early as possible, allowing you to focus on the next steps of your financial freedom journey.

Contributing as much as you can towards your pension, as early as you can, means that your money will do most of the hard work for you later on in life due to the magic of compound interest. As you embark on the next steps your financial freedom journey, you can take comfort that your retirement plans are progressing nicely. It also gives you options later down the line, for example, changing to a less stressful job with a lower salary, as your pension fund will be large enough such that compound interest will make it grow to a sufficient level that will provide you with your desired retirement income without needing to contribute another penny.

If, by the age of 40, you have amassed a pension pot worth £200,000, you stop making contributions and it earns a 5% annual return, by the time you are 67, you would have a pension pot worth c.£746,000 which would provide an annual income of just under £30,000! Alternatively, if you have a pension pot of £100,000 at age 40, you would have a pension pot of c.£373,000, providing an annual income of just under £15,000.

In each of these scenarios, you won't have to contribute another penny to your pension between the ages of 40 and 67. In theory, you can change to a less stressful job and take a reduction in your salary knowing you will have a sufficient income in your retirement even if you do nothing else.

To demonstrate what happens if you neglect your pension and have nothing invested at 40, assume you'll earn £30,000 per year and contribute 10% of your monthly salary into your pension from age 40 to 67. At 67, your pension pot would be valued at £164,000 and provide you with an income of just over £6,500 per year. Just to emphasise - you would have to work throughout this time, even if you hated your job. It is important not to be trapped in a job you don't like, just because you didn't invest in your pension from an early age.

Summary:
One of the benefits employers provide is pension contribution matching which gives you a 100% return on your money and you should maximise these contributions as early as possible to give yourself the best chance of building a sizeable pension fund in the background whilst you continue with the rest of your financial freedom journey.

By now, you should also appreciate how vital it is to contribute as much as possible to your pension as early as possible to take advantage of compound interest and give you options in the future, whether this means working a less stressful job or part time, starting your own business, or simply continuing as you are but knowing you can sleep at night in the comfort that you have a financially secure retirement. Make hay whilst the sun is shining and maximise those employer matches!

Key takeaways:
- Step 2 of the Framework is to maximise your employer's pension contributions.
- Employers can offer very generous pension contribution matches which is effectively free money, 100% returns, which is one of the best investments you can make.
- Reach out to your HR team to understand your

pension options and take advantage of them immediately.

Framework Step 3 - pay off consumer debt

Having followed Steps 1 and 2 of the Framework, you will now have one month's worth of expenses saved and be maximising your employer pension contributions. This puts you in a position to tackle the next Step of the Framework which is paying off your consumer debts. Your consumer debts include any credit cards, store cards, car loans/leases, buy now pay later loans...essentially everything but your mortgage. You should have a clear idea of your debts from undertaking your audit in Step 0, including the outstanding amounts, interest rates and any offer periods.

You should now turn your full Wealth Building Fund towards paying off debts. In parallel, you should be continually reviewing your expenses, renegotiating or switching to cheaper alternatives where possible to boost your WBF, as well as reviewing your possessions and selling any unwanted items to give you a one off bonus to help clear your debts as quickly as possible.

There are two schools of thought when approaching the repayment of debts, both of which require you to be paying the minimum amounts due on all of your debts (thereby avoiding penalty fees) and then focusing on paying off one debt at a time.

Debt 'avalanche':

This involves ranking your debts from highest interest rate to lowest and repaying the one with the highest interest rate first before moving on to and clearing the next highest, and so on until you are completely debt free. From a financial perspective, this is the most efficient method because it minimises the amount of interest you pay as you tackle each debt. A drawback is that it can be harder to build up momentum, especially if your debts with higher interest rates are attached to your larger debt balances, as they can take longer to clear down.

A debt avalanche can be a suitable method if you don't necessarily need the short term wins of repaying small balances (for example the motivation and discipline to stay the course and repay all of your debts). I personally recommend this method to my clients and often find a huge amount of momentum is built up once the most expensive debt has been repaid, the speed at which the remaining debts are repaid then tends to increase.

Debt 'snowball':

Rather than prioritising the repayment of debts based on the interest rate, the debt snowball method involves prioritising your debts from lowest value to highest value, paying the minimum amount due on all debts whilst directing the rest of your Wealth Building Fund towards repaying the smallest debt in full, and then moving on to the next smallest, and so on.

This method is very good for creating momentum compared

to the debt avalanche method where it can take a while to repay your first debt. I see this method as similar to climbing up a big hill whereby you build up speed at the bottom to gain momentum before the long ascent to the top. When using the snowball method to tackle smaller debts, it is important to remember that you could be accruing sizeable interest on your larger debts if they carry a higher interest rate.

There is no right or wrong method, as each has its own pros and cons; yes the debt avalanche is mathematically the option which means you will limit the amount of interest you pay, but using either method means you are prioritising debt repayment and are on the way to financial freedom.

If at all possible, you should really try and eliminate (or severely limit) your credit card spending and additional borrowing during this time, paying with cash wherever possible and if you do use a credit card, ensuring it is paid off in full each month. You want to focus your efforts on repaying existing debts and it can be difficult and demotivating if your outstanding balances keep increasing.

Ways to reduce the cost of debt:

As you embark on the debt repayment phase of your financial freedom journey, it is important to make every effort to minimise interest costs as this will not only mean you pay less interest, but it can help stabilise your outstanding debt balances too. A very effective method you can use to reduce interest payments on credit card debts is to consolidate your credit cards by doing a balance transfer. This involves moving your credit card debts on interest bearing accounts to a new credit card which has an interest free offer period. There are often fees involved in doing this which can be between 1-3%

of the balance you are transferring, but this can sometimes provide you with over 24 months of breathing space in which to attack the debt as it avoids interest accruing on the balance.

Be very careful with these cards because the offer terms vary significantly. For example, often, these cards are only interest free on balance transfers and not purchases which can attract very high interest rates, so only use them to park your balance whilst you repay it. Also, these facilities should only be used as a means to an end, a method to repay debts, not as an excuse to just buy more things whilst continually rolling over debts to new credit cards. As a rule, you should always balance transfer your interest bearing credit cards to 0% interest cards until all debts are repaid. Consolidating your debts is not only the best thing financially, but has enormous psychological benefits.

Whilst you are unable to balance transfer non-credit card debts, there could be an opportunity to consolidate multiple loans together into a single one. If you are genuinely struggling to repay your debts and there are no options to transfer such debt, you can try and negotiate with your lender. Explain that you are wanting to repay their loan and need some temporary help, such as a lower interest rate, repayment or interest holiday, to give yourself the best chance of getting rid of the debt. If you are in a position where you are unable to repay your debts, you should contact the National Debt Helpline[1] which is a government run service that will be able to advise and assist you. Burying your head in the sand is never the right answer, ultimately, your lenders want their money back and will usually be reasonable with you in reaching their objective. As with everything financial, you need to weigh up all available options and determine the best and most financially efficient for your circumstances.

Above all, remember, any windfall, cost savings and pay rises you receive during this Step 3 are to be contributed directly towards your Wealth Building Fund and subsequently pointed towards your debt repayments to get out of debt faster.

One of the toughest challenges in achieving financial freedom is to change your mindset so that consumer debt is no longer part of your life. This may seem very strange because we have been conditioned throughout our lives to believe that it is a normal thing to have credit card debts, store cards, car loans etc. and consumer credit is often the method used to fund the conspicuous purchases that have the social connotations that show others that we are doing well. The obsession of buying things with money you don't have to impress people you don't know needs to come to an end.

To demonstrate just how much holding consumer debt is engrained in our society, in the UK, only 22% of adults went into 2021 *without* any non-mortgage debt.[2] Becoming financially free involves rebelling against societies norms; adopting the mindset of using cash and saving up to buy the things you want, as opposed to being impatient and taking out credit to have the instant gratification of buying them now. Having to buy things with cash as opposed to debt means you will really appreciate the items you buy because of the thought and patience that went into the process. The behavioural shift of being patient and really appreciating the things you buy will help you never go into debt again.

In fact, what I have personally found by following the Framework is that I have realised that it is not *things* that make me happy but *time*, and control of that time. I am not stressed about having to succumb to the pressures of society to buy the latest phone, trainers, car, jacket or other fashion item, I take great comfort in focusing my efforts on buying time and am confident that, if you really think about it, you will feel the same.

Key takeaways:
- Consumer debt is a way of life in the UK, it is actually unusual to be debt free and so Step 3 of the Framework is to pay off your consumer debts.
- Use the debt avalanche or debt snowball method to tackle your debts, which involve making the minimum payments due on all debts and prioritising the repayment of the debt from either highest to lowest interest rate or smallest to largest balance, depending on your preference.
- Utilise balance transfers and consolidation loans to minimise interest payments and help stabilise debt balances to help you repay your balances faster.
- Don't be afraid to speak with your lenders if you are struggling to repay your debts, and if you are in a position where you are unable to repay your debts you should contact the National Debt Helpline.
- A change in mindset is required to break the cycle of consumer debt; stop normalising the use of debt to buy things, defer your gratification; save up and pay with cash.

Framework Step 4 - increase your emergency fund

This is the stage where you will begin to really build up a nice financial cushion giving you a sense of security you may never have felt before, knowing that no matter what the financial emergency, you will have enough protection to ride it out. As you will now have repaid all of your consumer debt (which is simply fantastic by the way!!), your full Wealth Building Fund should now be directed towards your emergency fund until it covers three to six months' worth of expenses.

The three to six month range should act as a guardrail between which your emergency fund should be maintained at all times. Whether you save towards the lower or higher end of this range should be influenced by the security of your employment; the more secure your job, the less you need to have saved, or the closer you are to retirement, the more you should have saved. Ultimately, the size of your fund is your choice and if you would feel more comfortable with two or nine months in your emergency fund, do this, the main thing is that you have enough of a financial cushion to withstand any financial shock.

You will recall that the rules and guidance in terms of what constitutes your monthly expenses, where to save your fund and what it should be used for were covered in Step 1, so I will not repeat them here. What I do want to emphasise though is that you should continually review your monthly expenses and reflect any changes in your emergency fund accordingly. For instance, if you renegotiate your car insurance, saving you £50 per month, this will automatically increase the number of months' cover you have saved. As discussed earlier, it is also vital that you review the market periodically for the best interest rates for your savings account and switch where appropriate - there is usually nothing to be gained from being loyal to your provider!

When you reach this stage, it may also be the only time in your life that you have not had consumer debt hanging over you and, if you don't maintain your self-discipline, it can be easy to neglect Step 4 and instead just go and spend the extra money from your Wealth Building Fund on non-wealth building activity. If you are tempted to stop your financial freedom journey at this point, then I encourage you to read (and re-read if necessary) the following facts which should help persuade you to stay the course.

In the UK, three in ten people have no savings at all and four in ten don't have sufficient savings to last one month without receiving a pay check, which[1] is staggering. Put another way, 70% of the UK population would be in serious trouble if they experienced a financial emergency! Being financially free means going against societies norms; I don't want you to follow the herd and get yourself into financial difficulty by buying unnecessary consumer goods, I want you to avoid this precarious situation and live life on your terms.

Consider this example: if a 30 year old's essential expenses were £2,000 per month and they had built up a six month emergency fund worth £12,000, they would be way ahead of most people in the UK, as you can see by the average savings by age range below:

Age Range	Average Savings[2]
25-34	£3,544
35-44	£6,000
45-54	£11,000
55+	£20,000

Society encourages us to continually compare ourselves to others in every aspect of our lives, but this is especially the case when it comes to how much money we have. It seems that as long as you look like you are doing well financially on the outside, it doesn't matter what is actually happening underneath. This is absurd. It is a bit like the difference between what people post on social media (a highlight reel of their lives) versus the reality of the rest of their life. Financial success is no different.

The elephant in the room when it comes to an emergency fund is that inflation will be eroding away at its value, due to the low interest rates that easy access savings accounts attract. Remember, your emergency fund is not there to make you rich, it is there to give you peace of mind and financial security, avoiding the need to turn to debt to fund unexpected events.

The main benefit of building your fund is, really, psychological; there is a mountain of research highlighting the negative impact that financial difficulty can have on one's mental health. The stress and anxiety caused by financial difficulty can be all-consuming, especially where debt becomes uncontrollable. The overwhelming feeling can make it harder to think clearly, perform in your job, maintain relationships and make sensible financial decisions, all of which further worsen a financial position, and the spiral continues. The idea of building up your emergency fund is to give you sufficient cover to never have to go into debt again and eliminate any worry about being financially paralysed by an unexpected expense. This peace of mind is indescribable; I remember the feeling I had when I built up my emergency fund and the day to day financial anxiety disappeared. I started to walk taller, felt more relaxed and had a real sense of achievement. The security has allowed me to now focus all of my mental efforts on the next steps of my own financial freedom journey which includes, among other things, writing this book and educating people on this life changing methodology.

Key takeaways:
- Step 4 of the Framework is to increase your emergency fund to cover you for between three and six months' worth of expenses.
- The three and six months is a guardrail and you can save more or less than this depending on your personal preferences.
- Building up a comfortable financial cushion is essential, not just for your mental health but to give you the springboard to continue on your journey to financial freedom.
- Regularly review your expenses and financial situation and adjust your emergency fund accordingly.
- In the event you need to use your emergency fund, divert the appropriate amount of your Wealth

Building Fund back to your emergency fund until it returns to your desired level.

The fork in the road: reach for your freedom

You have now reached the point where you have a solid emergency fund, no consumer debt and are maximising your employer pension contributions. At this stage, you are ready to start aggressively pursuing your financial freedom.

You know by now that you need to have at least 25 times your annual expenses in an investment portfolio in order to become financially free (and you should have a clear idea of what this number is). The three options for your Wealth Building Fund are now:

1. overpay your mortgage to eliminate your biggest expense as quickly as possible;
2. invest into a diversified portfolio; or
3. a combination of 1 and 2.

The path you choose is completely up to you and there is no correct answer. Paying off your mortgage will eliminate your biggest expense and significantly reduce the size of investment portfolio required to support you indefinitely. For instance, if your annual expenses are £30,000 with a mortgage, you would need a portfolio of £750,000 to support you, however, if your expenses are £18,000 without a mortgage, you would only need £450,000. Reducing your living expenses also opens up other options which are unavailable if you have a sizeable house payment to make each month, such as only having to work part time or working in a less stressful job.

The alternative option to aggressively overpaying your mortgage is to divert your full WBF to your investment portfolio. As the rate of return you will earn investing will likely outweigh the interest rate on your mortgage (on average), it can make sense from a purely financial perspective to prioritise investing over mortgage overpayments. As we saw from the example above, choosing this route means you will need to save up more in order to cover your higher living expenses but it means your portfolio will grow much faster than with option one.

The third option is to both overpay your mortgage and invest in a diversified portfolio; this is the path I follow. By allocating part of your WBF to mortgage overpayments and part to your investment portfolio, you are eliminating your largest living expense whilst building your portfolio.

Ultimately, this is a personal choice and what you do depends on what financial freedom means for you and there is no rule to say you can't change your mind once you have started on a path; life happens and circumstances change, so it is important to regularly review your financial plans and objectives and ensure your actions are aligned to this.

The next two chapters explore these options in more detail as Step 5 and Step 6 of the Framework (respectively). I have also provided some worked examples which walk through how the different options can work in practice.

Framework Step 5 - attack your mortgage

At this stage of your financial freedom journey, you have reached what may be the most rewarding part of the journey; clearing your mortgage. You have worked so hard to understand your financial situation, repay your consumer debts, build up a solid financial buffer in the form of your emergency fund and made the tough decision to defer gratification by investing heavily into your pension, and you should be so proud of yourself! You now need to maintain this momentum by channelling your full Wealth Building Fund to overpaying your mortgage.

Mortgages are often seen as a badge of honour in society. You picture the happy couple clinking champagne glasses on social media when they purchase their first house (me included) but what is often overlooked is that having a mortgage is not the same as owning a home. Owning a home means you own 100% of the house, every brick and blade of grass is yours, not the bank's. When you have a mortgage, the bank owns the proportion of the house you don't which you gradually buy back from them (and then some!).

Your mortgage is likely to be your largest monthly expense and, therefore, clearing it, presents the biggest opportunity to increase your WBF and speed up your timeframe for achieving financial freedom. Clearing your mortgage will also mean your emergency fund will instantly last you a lot longer (given your mortgage will have been included in your calculation for building up your emergency fund in the first place), providing even more security. For example, if your expenses are £1,500 per month, of which £750 is your mortgage (note, the UK average is £733 per month)[1], a six month emergency fund would be £9,000 but as soon as this mortgage is cleared, the same £9,000 would last you 12 months.

There is an argument to delay repaying a mortgage because interest rates are at historic lows; why pay off the mortgage at 2.5% interest when you could invest at 7%? This is a good question, to which the answer varies depending on opinion, but my response based on my opinion is threefold. Firstly, it is simply *because* interest rates are at historic lows that you should overpay your mortgage; there has never been a better (and cheaper) time to do this and the faster you can do it, the less risk there is of being hit by higher interest rates in the future. Secondly, and more importantly in my opinion, there are huge psychological benefits of not having the pressure to meet a monthly mortgage payment, as you will be afforded immense freedom, the likes of which you will not have felt before. Thirdly, there is no guarantee that your health and wellbeing will keep up with the timeframe of your mortgage repayments, you may not be able to work in the same high pressure job twenty years from now to meet your repayments, so following Step 5 will enable you to eliminate this pressure from your life as early as possible.

The freedoms afforded to you from owning a home outright is the main motivation to make this commitment in the first place. From this point on, you will only have to meet your basic living expenses, which could mean a change in career to something which perhaps isn't as well paid but better aligns to your moral values. Or if you enjoy and want to continue your career and perhaps increase your earning potential, it means your WBF will be supercharged and you can invest aggressively into a portfolio to generate significant passive income. It could mean, for example, you can start your own business without the added stress and pressure of having to meet a monthly mortgage repayment and you can truly focus on growing the company in the right way for you. It also gives you the option to sell and take the equity out of your property, potentially to downsize or relocate to another part of the country, freeing up money to invest in a portfolio in the process, especially if you only live where you do for employment. I hope just these few options provide a spark of motivation for you as they do for me, but the options really are endless so focus on what motivates you and make it happen.

A word of warning, overpaying your mortgage does go against the grain of societal norms and, as your friends and family may instead choose to spend their money on other, overtly fancier things like exotic holidays and new cars, it can make it harder to be disciplined at this step. But just smile and get on with the overpayments, reminding yourself of your motivations and the inevitable deferred gratification, it will be more than worth it in the end.

If you are thinking, *how much difference can overpaying the mortgage really make?* or, *surely on such a long term and expensive debt, small overpayments won't matter at all?*, below are two examples that illustrate what difference even small additional contributions can make to your mortgage, it really is amazing.

Firstly, let's look at a 30 year, £250,000 mortgage with a 2.5% interest rate; the normal monthly repayment is £998, meaning the total amount repaid is just over £355,000; £250,000 of this is the principal and £105,000 is interest. The graph below shows the value of the outstanding mortgage if you were to overpay by just £100, £200, or £300 per month:

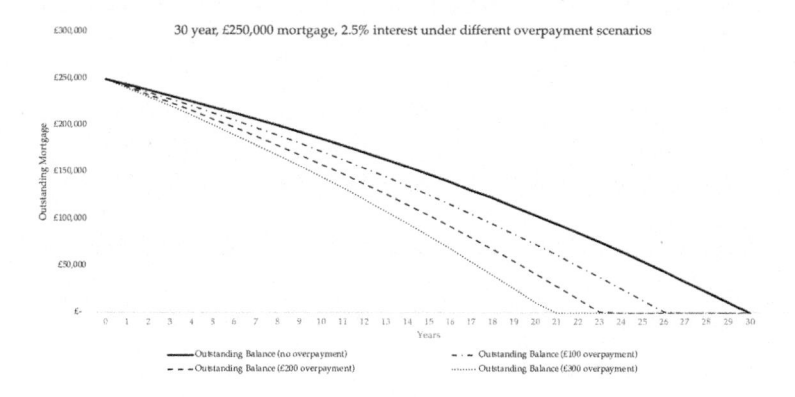

As you can see, if you could find an extra £100 per month to pay towards your mortgage:
- your mortgage would be cleared in just over 26 years, thereby giving you 4 years of your life back; and
- your total repayments over this period would be just over £340,000, saving you c.£15,000.

If you were to overpay by £300 per month, your mortgage would be cleared in just under 21 years and your interest repayments over the term of the mortgage would reduce by almost £35,000!

The results are even more impressive when you apply the same methodology to a larger mortgage balance, as we see below in our second example of a 25 year, £350,000 mortgage with a 3.5% interest rate; the normal monthly repayment is £1,753, meaning the total amount repaid is £525,836, of which £175,836 is purely interest.

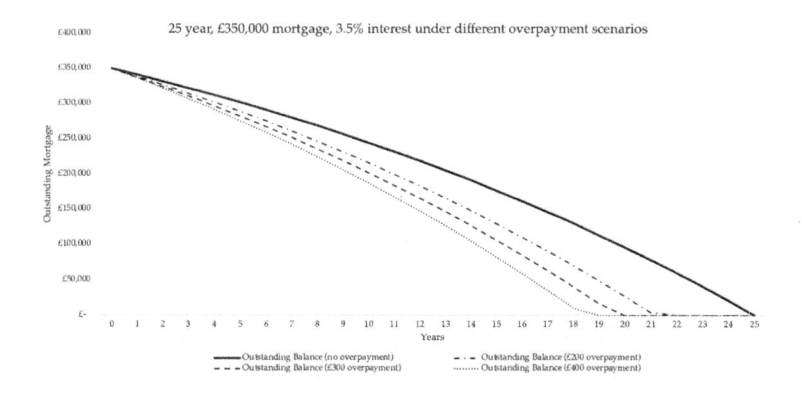

25 year, £350,000 mortgage, 3.5% interest under different overpayment scenarios

If you were able to overpay by £200 per month then you would have paid off your mortgage in just over 21 years and saved c.£29,000 in interest. Not only this, but the time you save means 4 years' less worry about interest rates rising or not having to stay in a job you don't like purely to meet your mortgage obligation.

Whilst both of these examples assume a constant interest rate throughout the term of the mortgage, which is unlikely to be the case in reality, I hope they highlight the exponential impact that small overpayments can make and the corresponding life changing consequences. I am assuming in all of these scenarios that you would prefer to be doing something else with your time other than your nine to five job and the Framework is designed to get you to this position in as quick a time as possible. If you are in a job you love, can't see yourself doing anything else and are happy to spend the next 25-30 years working for an employer then I commend you and you could sacrifice overpaying your mortgage to spend your Wealth Building Fund on other things. That said, I don't know many people that want to wake up every morning for the next 25 to 30 years for the daily grind, and I've never met anyone who regretted paying off their mortgage early.

Practicalities of overpaying your mortgage:

There are numerous ways you can overpay your mortgage, including simply overpaying each month to the value of your WBF, either as a one-off payment or direct debit, or, if you prefer not to overpay monthly, by saving up your WBF to make a one off lump-sum payment which offers some additional flexibility. Arranging recurring or one-off overpayments is very easy. A key thing to watch out for is that there is often an overpayment allowance (usually 10% of your outstanding balance) which restricts how much you can overpay. For instance, if your outstanding mortgage is £200,000 and you have a 10% overpayment allowance, you will only be allowed to overpay £20,000 before incurring penalties, so you should be careful not to exceed this amount.

Alternatively, you could look to reduce the term of your mortgage at the point you remortgage, by increasing your monthly repayment to an amount equal to your current repayment amount plus your WBF. For example, if your current mortgage repayment is £1,000 per month and, after following Steps 0-4, your WBF is £500, you could ether pay an extra £500 per month towards your mortgage, or remortgage so that your monthly repayments become £1,500 and your mortgage term reduced. There is usually a mortgage arrangement fee (normally around £1,000) attached to re-mortgaging, but you will be able to lock in an interest rate if you opt for a fixed rate mortgage and it can ensure you don't breach any existing overpayment allowance. The main drawback to reducing your mortgage term however, is that you are contractually bound to make the higher payment and lack the flexibility that comes with electing to overpay. A solution to this is that you can of course use a combination of the two options: re-mortgaging to slightly increase your repayments and reduce the term and then overpaying a one off amount as you see fit or if you receive a windfall.

Whichever route you take, overpaying your mortgage is a key milestone in your financial freedom journey, eventually relieving you of the pressure of having to meet monthly mortgage repayments and opening up a plethora of life changing options for you.

Summary:

Step 5 of the Framework is to attack your mortgage. I know attack sounds like a strong word, but your mortgage is the one big hurdle between you and your ability to grow significant wealth. Once you reach Step 5, not only is it your biggest expense, it is the one thing financially that truly dictates your life. The longer you have a mortgage, the longer you are trapped in your 9-5 job, not taking risks or doing what you want to do with your life, the more interest you are paying to your lender and the longer they control you.

Once you have paid for your house, have no other debt, your pension pot is increasing nicely and you have a healthy emergency fund, you will have a financial fortress, and this is where the dream of financial freedom can soon become a reality.

Key takeaways:
- Step 5 involves allocating your full WBF towards overpaying your mortgage.
- Paying off your mortgage eliminates your largest monthly expense, significantly reducing the amount of money you need invested in order to support your lifestyle.
- Small overpayments can make a massive difference to the length of your mortgage and the interest expense.
- Overpay by either:
  - officially reducing the mortgage term by increasing your monthly repayment to the sum of your current repayment plus your WBF; or
  - making regular or one-off overpayments of an amount equal to the value of your WBF, being aware of, and not exceeding, the maximum overpayment allowance.

Framework Step 6 - invest, invest, invest

The key to achieving your financial freedom is to ensure that your investments provide sufficient income to cover your living expenses indefinitely, and, as such, Step 6 of the Framework is to aggressively invest until the sum of your investments reaches the amount required to support your desired lifestyle, whether this be enough to enable you to work part time with investment income supplementing your employment income, or to never have to work again whilst travelling around the world in first class.

When I talk about investing to achieve financial freedom, there are various investment options available, in addition to investing in the financial markets, that can generate passive income. One such option is buy to let property, a common asset class in the UK, which we will explore later on in this book. Which option is best boils down to personal preference (I for one prefer, and am more comfortable with, investing in the financial markets) but, ultimately, whichever option you choose, the aim of the game is the same: to generate enough passive income to support your desired lifestyle, and you need to make a balanced and informed decision as to how to get there.

* * *

As stressed many times, you need to have 25 times your annual expenses saved in an investment portfolio to enable you to draw down 4% of your portfolio without running out of money and be financially free. If you have followed the Framework Steps sequentially, you will now be completely debt free, have a sizeable Wealth Building Fund and, consequently, be in a position to supercharge your investments. To put this into perspective and give you focus, the graph below gives you an indication of the amount required in an investment portfolio to support various income levels:

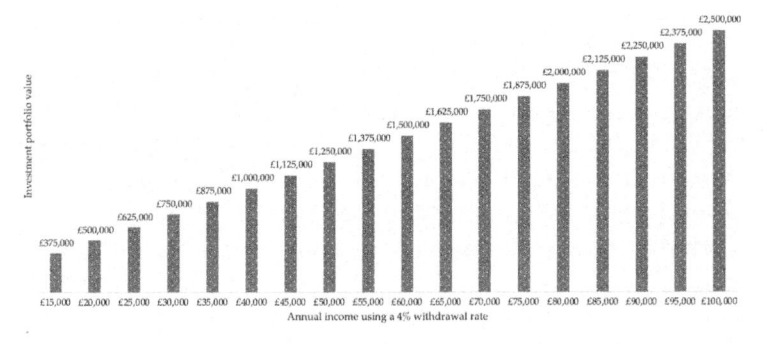

In terms of where to invest, as you ideally need to be earning an average long term return of at least 4% plus inflation, you typically should have a higher allocation towards riskier assets such as equities and property rather than bonds and cash. Naturally these types of investments are more volatile, however they increase the likelihood of achieving this required level of return, especially in the current low interest rate environment. That said, everyone's risk profile and tolerance vary and should be considered holistically in line with personal circumstance and situation. An Independent Financial Adviser can help you work out what's best for you.

It is also important to consider the value of your pension in these calculations, as it could mean that you won't need as much in your investment portfolio if you can survive on a lower income until the point you can access your pension. Consider this example: you are currently 45 and have a pension, accessible to you from age 55, which would give you an annual income of £10,000, and you have an investment portfolio of £300,000 which currently provides you with an annual income of £12,000. If you could survive on this income for 10 years, you wouldn't have to work from age 45 to 55 in the comfort that in 10 years, you can almost double your income. That said, rather than rely on investment income as their sole source of income, many people use it to supplement their lifestyle, making up any difference between their actual income from any work they choose to continue to do and their desired income... the possibilities are endless.

How you go about investing is up to you. Technology has made it much easier than it used to be; what previously required expensive Financial Advisers and Brokers now relies on robots to invest and rebalance portfolios automatically on your behalf for a nominal fee. I always recommend retaining control of your own portfolio, avoiding expensive fees whilst teaching you an invaluable life skill. Remember, if you intend to access the income from your portfolio before the time when you can access your pension account (which I assume is the case), then your investments should sit outside of your main employer pension in an account such as a Stocks and Shares ISA or taxable investment account.

Can you coast to financial freedom?
The simple answer is yes. Once you get to this stage of your journey, you will be free of your consumer debt, and, if you followed Step 5 and have cleared your mortgage, your monthly expenses will be a fraction of what they were

beforehand. It could also well be that you have saved enough into your employer pension and investment portfolio that, if you were to never invest another penny, you could retire at a more usual retirement age (e.g. 67) with the lifestyle you want. This is known as 'coasting financial freedom' and means all you have to do is have enough income to be able to support your existing lifestyle expenses until such time as you can access your pension savings. Whilst you won't have complete financial freedom at this point (i.e. your accessible investments are not enough to provide you with the passive income needed to fully support you), what you will have are options, for example to perhaps change employer, work part time or even start your own business. As long as you can sustain yourself, you can change your lifestyle knowing that you will have enough income to support your desired lifestyle in the future; you can take it easy and coast towards your financial freedom.

To illustrate how this works in practice, let's work through an example: assume you are 45 years old and have £200,000 saved in an employer pension, your monthly take-home pay is £3,000, you are completely debt free and your monthly expenses are £1,500. As a result, you live a great, happy life. Assume you leave your pension untouched and it grows at 4% annually after inflation until you want to draw it from age 67. By the time you are 67, your pension pot would be worth just under £474,000, which would provide an annual income of c.£19,000 (assuming you withdrew 4% annually). As you only need £1,500 per month to sustain your lifestyle and, at 45, earn £3,000, you have the option to take a lower salary in a different, perhaps less stressful and more fulfilling, full time job, you could work full time for six months of the year and take six months per year off, work part time in the same job or do something completely different. The beauty of coasting financial freedom is that you have options. You have options because you worked hard early on to take care of and create those options for your future self.

The drawback with coasting financial freedom is that you do need to continue working, whether this be working for yourself or for someone else, to sustain your living expenses, as opposed to being able to rely entirely on your investments to fund your expenses and literally sit on the beach doing nothing for the rest of your life if you desired. To be clear, this isn't an either/or decision, as this stage can quickly lead to full financial freedom if you continue aggressively saving and investing, but I wanted to highlight that there is an option to get off the ride here, if it means you are able to live the life you want and be fulfilled.

I'd like to stay on the ride, so what do I need to do to get full financial freedom?

You simply need to keep investing until you reach the target fund value of 25 times your expenses to achieve complete financial freedom. In order to attain this goal, it is important to have a clear idea of what this number is so you can track your progress, keep momentum and, most importantly, know when you get there! If you need £500,000 for your desired lifestyle, there is little point, in my opinion, in continuing in the rat race once you have achieved this.

I personally don't see full financial freedom as being the golden ticket that allows you to just sit in your pants watching boxsets from the point you achieve it until you die (although my girlfriend would likely disagree); I see it as the epitome of freedom, freedom to do something meaningful with your life. Perhaps you have always wanted to live by the sea or in the countryside, or work in a more rewarding career helping people, but you haven't been in the financial position to be able to do so. No matter what your dreams, earning passive income from an investment portfolio to sustain you will help you transform your dreams into reality – and who doesn't want that?

It is also at this point that you can really reap the benefits of having increased your income through ongoing improvements to your skills and education (more on this in the next chapter). By the time you get to this stage of the journey, you will likely be approaching your maximum earning power, so all of the elements of serious wealth building coincide to create the perfect storm; you are earning the most you've ever earned and your essential living expenses are minimal. You are in the prime position to maximise your investments.

Summary:
Step 6 of your financial freedom journey involves directing all of your Wealth Building Fund towards your investment portfolio until you have enough in your account to provide sufficient income for your desired lifestyle.

It is important to remember that you don't have to have paid off your mortgage before you start investing, this just means that you will have to work for longer, potentially in a job you despise, to achieve your financial goals. The benefits of simultaneously investing and paying off your mortgage are that you will have built up a nice portfolio by the time you become debt free and will have generated a solid knowledge base of, and years of experience in, investing, which will be extremely useful when you come to channelling your full WBF towards your portfolio (i.e. when you do eventually relieve yourself of your mortgage debt).

* * *

As the route to financial freedom is different for everyone, and will most likely change throughout your life depending on your circumstances at a particular time, it is important to review your approach regularly. In addition, the lifestyle you thought you wanted as a 50 year old when you were 25, may be very different when you are 35. It is a personal journey with ups and downs, but the key thing is to maintain discipline and focus on your end goal (whatever this ends up looking like). Remember, no matter whether you decide to invest once you have *cleared* your mortgage, or whilst you are *clearing* your mortgage, you will be so much more financially successful than you would have been if you didn't follow this Framework.

I will also re-emphasise here that being financially free and retiring early does not necessarily equate to lazing around all day watching TV; it is designed to give you back valuable time and the option to live life on your terms and, if you desire, make a positive, fulfilling, difference to you and those around you.

Key takeaways:
- Step 6 of the Framework involves aggressively investing in your well diversified portfolio until you have 25 times your annual expenses invested.
- Ensure you review your investments and goals regularly because you could be in a position to coast to financial freedom whereby you no longer need to invest in either your pension or portfolio in order to secure your desired income at retirement age, as long as you can fund your existing living expenses until retirement.

Ongoing activities for financial freedom

Underpinning each stage of your financial freedom journey are various ongoing activities, or 'core behaviours', that are central to individual success; from taking out and maintaining appropriate insurance, to maintaining a budget, developing yourself and increasing your earning power (and WBF). Whilst achieving financial freedom relies on adherence to the specifics of the Framework, it is vital to also remember that such ongoing activities should be carried out concurrently throughout your life. Some of these activities are outlined below.

Protect yourself and your loved ones:

We don't like to think about bad things happening to us, such as critical illness, accidents or even death but, unfortunately, these events are part of life and it is important that we protect ourselves against them. Having appropriate insurance in place (e.g. car, home, contents and life insurance) provides you and your loved ones with peace of mind for worst case scenarios.

In terms of the type and level of insurance cover required, this comes down to personal circumstance. For example; fully comprehensive car insurance might be most appropriate for someone who frequently uses their car and/or has a newer model; someone with higher outgoings, such as an expensive mortgage, could expect to have higher life insurance cover; and someone who owns their home or has a mortgage, should have buildings insurance to cover the cost of any essential repairs and maintenance. Having insurance doesn't remove the hassle of having to sort out any problems, but it does relieve you of the stress and worry that comes with it.

As with all financial products, it is vital to shop around for the most appropriate cover at the best available price and cash back websites often give significant rewards for shopping for insurance products through them too.

Develop yourself:
Self-development, in my opinion, is the single most significant contributor to success in life. You are your biggest asset and generator of income; whether you are employed or run your own company, you are the one responsible for how much you earn and how successful you can be.

Developing yourself comes in many forms but one of the most significant is your level of formal education, being a key determinant of your income. The graph below is a few years old but remains a helpful illustration of the average salary of someone in the UK by formal qualification level.[1]

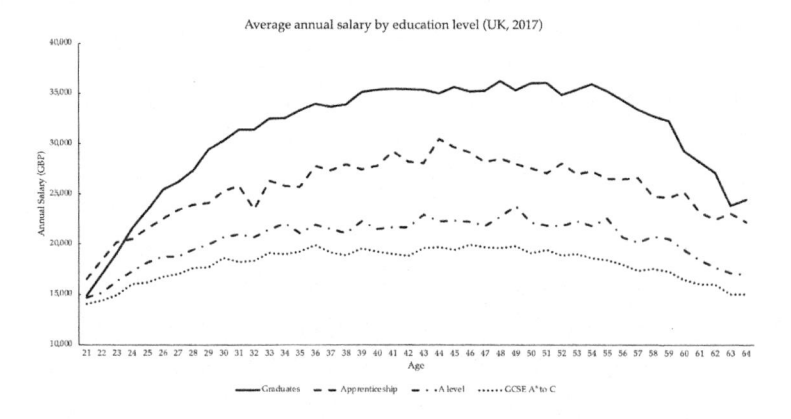

Average annual salary by education level (UK, 2017)

——— Graduates — — Apprenticeship — · · A level ······· GCSE A* to C

As you can clearly see, typically the higher the level of your education, the higher your income. It therefore goes without saying that to maximise your income level, you should aim to get the highest level of education possible. Although undertaking a full time University course is the standard route to higher education, it is not the only way and is not always an option for many people; there are numerous alternatives, with many Universities offering online only and part time study, meaning it is never too late to achieve additional qualifications plus you can continue earning money whilst studying, which, given the rising cost of education, could be a valuable alternative for even more people in the future.

Before you embark on your University journey, you do of course need to determine whether the career you aspire to have requires a degree and choose your course very carefully, especially with the cost of a degree (currently £9,000 per year, not including living expenses). Choosing a degree in a subject that increases your chances of landing a higher paying job, for example, finance, law, medicine, dentistry, engineering or computer science, is sensible and increasingly common, as such increases your graduate prospects (including your ability to repay the debt accrued during your studies!). Ultimately, education is a financial and time investment, so you need to make sure it pays off.

In addition to University education, there are specialist professional qualifications which are a huge time commitment but can mean your income prospects are stratospheric. For example, I pursued the Chartered Institute of Management Accountant (CIMA) qualification once I finished University, which led to me more than doubling my salary in a matter of years and provides a solid income trajectory from here on. If you have the appropriate foundation qualifications and the ability to pursue a professional qualification, the return on investment is huge, although it does require sacrifices with a lot of evening and weekend work, making it extremely worthwhile but exhausting. Employers may be able to support with professional qualifications by contributing to the cost of exams and courses and/or giving you additional time off to study, so it's worth exploring your options.

Outside of formal education, you can continue to develop yourself by reading books on relevant topics that will help increase your income and earning power, whether this be related to your work or personal finance, investing, building businesses or autobiographies of successful entrepreneurs and other inspirational people. There is so much material online and so many books available, meaning you can literally teach yourself anything. I have embraced self-education throughout my life and, similar to money, knowledge compounds over time and, once you have read and read some more on a certain topic, you will be amazed at how much you know. In addition to written material, there are some great online platforms for training courses (such as udemy.com) where you can learn about a wide variety of topics, taught by experts, which are really engaging and cost effective, some even give you formal certifications!

Self-development and self-education should not be underestimated as a tool, beyond your formal education, to help you generate the required knowledge that gives you the best chance of increasing your income and Wealth Building Fund.

Track your finances:
There is a saying in business which is pertinent to your personal finances, 'if you can't measure it, you can't manage it'. If achieving financial freedom is one of your goals (which I assume is correct given you are reading this) then you need to get into the habit of measuring or 'tracking' your finances on an ongoing basis, a ritual, if you will.

Tracking your finances involves carrying out the following:
- ✓ Calculating your assets and liabilities
- ✓ Setting your objectives - i.e. repaying debt, saving for retirement, overpaying your mortgage, etc.
- ✓ Building an annual budget, split by month, which will enable you to achieve your objectives
- ✓ Reviewing your progress against your budget each month and taking corrective action where needed
- ✓ Reviewing your objectives every 6-12 months and adjusting your budgets and activities accordingly

Although this may sound onerous and intimidating initially, what you are doing is providing structure, direction and discipline to your finances. Knowing your target wealth building fund, how much you need to save or the amount of debt to repay each month to achieve your financial goals, will mean you don't drift with your money choices. I find that having a set day each month dedicated to tracking my finances is very helpful (I use pay day), as I know that, on that day, I pay out every penny of my income towards the activities that are directed towards achieving my objectives.

Setting a budget and tracking your spend should not stop the moment you achieve financial freedom; it is a process that should continue indefinitely to achieve and then ensure you maintain your freedom (and stopping you from spending your lifetime's income in just a few years). Despite your initial reaction to the idea of tracking your finances, I promise that you will soon start to get excited about it; you will get a real buzz from seeing tangible progress towards meeting your goals. To add additional motivation, you could reward yourself with something once you have achieved an objective. For example, when you have repaid all of your consumer debts, treat yourself to that nice meal out, or those new jeans (paying with cash of course!).

Summary:

Throughout your journey to financial freedom, it is important to have your house in order and remove surplus stress, including protecting yourself through appropriate insurance; tracking your progress; and improving your biggest asset - you - through formal education, professional qualifications, and informal training courses. These ongoing activities are intended to help you form the habit of continual self-development and improvement, ultimately increasing your Wealth Building Fund to accelerate you towards financial freedom.

Key takeaways:
- The following ongoing activities underpin Steps 0-6 of the Framework and are just as important:
    - Protecting yourself and your loved ones through appropriate insurance
    - Continuously tracking your financial position and progress towards your financial freedom goals
    - Focusing on self-development through formal and informal education to increase your knowledge and earning firepower

Increasing your Wealth Building Fund

As you have read throughout this book, your Wealth Building Fund is your tool to becoming financially free and you should be focussed on trying to increase it wherever and whenever possible. As your WBF is simply your income less your expenses, you can increase your WBF by earning more income, decreasing expenses, or, the best solution, doing both.

Ways to increase your income:
Unlike expenses for which there is a floor (as you always need a certain amount of money to live), income potential is infinite and you should aim to increase income whenever you can. Although any extra income is great, you should try and generate income which does not directly rely on your time in order to earn it.

Ask for a pay rise (well, if you don't ask...):
On the road to generating additional income, asking your current employer for a pay rise is often overlooked but this can be your biggest and quickest source of additional income. Are you consistently over-performing and going above and beyond the call of duty? Or could you discuss taking on additional responsibilities in exchange for higher pay? If so,

put forward a business case to your manager to pitch for your pay rise.

There is a balance of power between you and your employer; they pay you in exchange for the delivery of services using your specialist knowledge and skills. As you learn and grow in an organisation, your ability to deliver will increase and you may have received pay rises to reflect this. However, if your skills have grown and are worth more than the pay you currently receive, i.e. you are giving your employer more value than the money you receive in exchange, this difference is what you want to focus on in order to secure a pay rise.

It is always a good idea to research what the average pay for your role is by consulting resources such as Glassdoor and LinkedIn and speaking to specialist recruiters in your particular industry or field to get a really good understanding of the salary ranges you could expect for the types of responsibilities you have. It is also prudent to have a bank of examples of where you have over-delivered, a list of deliverables that would be at risk if you were to leave, and a note of the specialist skills and knowledge you have that warrant a pay rise. It is also important to remember that it would cost your employer a lot of money to replace you and there would be a period of lost productivity whilst your replacement is up-skilled; the case for paying you more money to stay can be quite compelling.

Remember, you always have the option to sell your services to another employer for a higher price and thus walk away from your current employer if you are unable to secure a pay rise. Your employer will take whatever you are willing to give, so you need to make sure you are being sufficiently rewarded in the trade.

***

Gain additional qualifications:
Another way of increasing your pay is to increase your level of qualification. If you are in a career which has professional qualifications, such as accountancy, law, engineering or procurement, you could study for a professional qualification in your spare time. Although it takes significant commitment, it is well worth the money; I studied for a Diploma in Corporate Treasury in my spare time for three years which led me to enhance my career and earning prospects over and above my already solid prospects as a Chartered Management Accountant. I found it incredibly rewarding, as it not only increased my future earning potential, but I also developed a number of transferable skills and habits in the process.

Overtime:
If you have the opportunity in your job to work overtime then a quick and easy way to boost your WBF is to work as much overtime as you can. Speak to your manager and let them know that you are keen to work overtime – present it as a win-win: you earn some more money, your employer is relieved of staffing pressure.

Your employment is your main source of income and so you need to maximise it until you have enough invested so you no longer have to rely on it. Asking for a pay rise and overtime, changing to an employer who will pay you more for your services, continually researching and monitoring your income situation and investing in professional education are all ways of increasing your income.

The 'gig economy' and side businesses:
If working overtime or extra shifts for your current

employer is not an option for you, there has never been a time with as many opportunities to earn additional income from other sources (although do double check for any restrictions in your employment contract first!).

The boom of the 'gig economy' means that you can sign up to work for companies such as Uber, Deliveroo, Just Eat etc. in an instant and be working a few hours outside of your main employment and earning extra money in no time. For instance, earning an extra £15 three times per week would generate £180 per month, or £2,160 per year which can make big inroads to your wealth building. Whilst not a scalable job (i.e. your income is limited to the number of hours you work) and likely not a sustainable route to achieving financial freedom, utilising the 'gig' method can be useful if you need to urgently pay down debt or rebuild an emergency fund.

Another option if you are in a profession or have a skill set that allows you to do so, is to build a business in your spare time which could increase your income and may even be the vehicle that enables you to achieve financial freedom. If you are a hairdresser currently working for an employer, could you also cut hair in your spare time under your own brand name? If you are a lawyer, could you provide training to LPC students, via a YouTube channel for example? Are you a gifted musician who could offer lessons in evenings and weekends? There may be endless options available to you but you should aim to earn income from a venture that can be scaled in the future and doesn't require your time to increase income, e.g. once you have a video on YouTube, it doesn't take any more of your time whether you have one viewer or ten million. Even if your business takes a while to get off the ground or isn't as successful as you expected, don't be disheartened, persevere; you will still be developing new skills such as sales, customer service, product development, website building, money management, marketing, communication and countless others, which will only benefit you and help you build on your success in the future! Remember that the most successful business people likely didn't get it right first time!

Ways to reduce your expenses:

As mentioned at the outset of this chapter, in addition to increasing your income, the other lever to increase your WBF is to reduce your expenses. There are various ways to save money, too many to cover here, but I wanted to touch on some effective methods I have personally used and continue to implement to consistently reduce my costs.

Evaluate every expense:

It is important to think carefully about your expenses to ensure that, firstly, they are absolutely necessary, and secondly, you are getting maximum value from them. There are a number of considerations prior to spending money:

1. evaluate the opportunity cost of the purchase (i.e. how much of a return would I get if I invested this money instead?)
2. ask yourself how much time it would take to earn the money to pay for the item (i.e. is this thing really worth X hours of my time?)
3. for larger purchases, wait 24 hours before making your decision

Admittedly I don't do this with every item on my grocery list but for everything else I do. I also ask myself the following questions: am I comfortable with the true cost of the item? Is it in my budget? Do I actually need it? Will it add value to my life? Only if the answer is yes, do I buy it. I have found this 'internal approval' process really effective when I am tempted to buy something that falls outside of my typical month to month spending. I have saved hundreds, if not thousands, of pounds over the years by just not giving in to impulse and unnecessary spending.

Learn to cook and embrace batch cooking:

After your housing and essential travel costs, food is likely one of your largest monthly costs and therefore presents a great opportunity to save money and increase your WBF without sacrificing your quality of life. I know for many, cooking is seen as a chore and the temptation to buy processed ready meals, order takeaway or order pre-prepared food boxes is all too much, leading to spending an extortionate amount on something that can easily be created by yourself. Cooking healthy, wholesome food is so much easier than it may seem and, I promise, if you watch a few cookery programmes or invest in a few cook books, it will feel like less and less of a chore as time goes on. You may even get the bug and never look back.

Your initial reaction may be 'this is all well and good, but I have no time for cooking'. The easiest way to change this is to invest in a slow cooker. With minutes of preparation and some forward planning you can make the most wonderful meals including curries, stews and soups. As an example, one of our favourite meals is a paneer and spinach curry which takes 10 minutes to prepare before going into the slow cooker for six hours whilst I am at work. I then portion it into Tupperware and freeze; typically producing eight portions of food at a time and costing less than £1 per portion. I find spending a few hours batch cooking at the weekend for the week ahead makes a huge difference, especially when weeks turn out to be particularly busy. I design my weekday menus such that only rice, noodles or pasta needs to be cooked to compliment the pre-prepared meal, avoiding the temptation to order in at the last minute.

Create a meal plan and shop smart:

Creating a weekly meal plan in combination with a shopping list is a really effective way to save money; it stops you overspending on your groceries as you know exactly what you need to buy, thereby eliminating buying surplus food and ultimately wasting it. As well as being good for your wallet, it is a good thing for the planet too.

In a similar vein, consider shopping in discount supermarkets or foregoing expensive brands in favour of buying supermarket own brands; the cost is often better than half price when compared to the main brands and the quality tends to be just as good (usually because the big named brands also produce the supermarket branded products!). For example, some supermarkets are now selling 'wonky' veg at a significantly lower price than its 'perfect' counterpart, which would otherwise go to landfill purely because it doesn't meet some unnecessary societal standard. Please consider adding a mis-shaped carrot to your basket instead of the perfectly straight one; pay half the price and do your bit to give the planet half a chance.

Geographical arbitrage:

This concept centres around taking advantage of the different income levels and living expenses of two separate locations by living in a location where it is cheaper to live, whilst earning a relatively higher salary from a different location, thereby maximising the profitability of your employment, for example, working in a high paying job for a London based firm but living in, and working remotely from a cheaper part of the country. I have heard of people taking this arbitrage to an extreme by working as freelancers for European businesses whilst living in and travelling across South East Asia.

It seems likely that there will be more opportunities to take advantage of geographical arbitrage over the coming years following the COVID-19 pandemic, as employers become even more accepting of employees not being physically located in the office combined with the increased confidence that technology is good enough for people to operate seamlessly remotely. It is worth considering whether geographical arbitrage is a viable option for you, as it could make a massive difference to your quality of life as well as your bank balance (of course, you will only feel the full effect of geographical arbitrage if you add the extra money generated to your Wealth Building Fund and channel it towards wealth building activity!).

Embrace DIY:
Whenever you need jobs doing around the house, it can be tempting to hire the services of a specialist who will, typically, charge you an extortionate fee. Usually, these jobs are actually fairly straight forward and something you could do yourself with some guidance from YouTube videos and the right tools. My girlfriend and I recently repainted every wall, door and ceiling in our house, as well as renovated the garden, saving thousands of pounds and developing new skills in the process. Seeing the transformation was extremely rewarding and I have gained the confidence to now tackle anything that needs doing around the house.

That said, there are some jobs for which you need and should seek the services of a professional, either because they are too complicated and time consuming to do yourself or require formal certification, such as gas or electrics.

DIY also extends to the more common and mundane tasks such as cleaning, doing your own ironing and washing your own car. The more tasks you can do yourself, the more money you can put towards your wealth building fund and the faster your journey to financial freedom. Think twice about whether you can do a task yourself before hiring someone else to do it for you. The only compelling caveat to this is if you could earn more money doing something else during the time that you would otherwise be doing your chores, than it costs to hire someone else to do them. For instance, if you could earn £15 per hour and it costs £10 per hour to hire a cleaner, in theory you should hire the cleaner and use the time to earn £5 profit. This logic is sound as long as you can actually use that time to earn money, i.e. you do some work for a client whilst your house is being cleaned.

Company loyalty doesn't pay off:
Companies don't care about how long you have been one of their customers, they only care about maximising new customers (acquisitions) and minimising the number of customers that leave them (churn); the reason being is that they like to demonstrate to their shareholders how much their business is growing. When your introductory offers expire and you have to start paying the premium 'non-offer' rates, this is the point at which companies begin to take notice of your tenure.

If you haven't already done so, now is the time to get out of the mentality that companies reward loyalty. Instead, you can use a company's lack of loyalty to your advantage; whenever your contracts for utilities, phone, insurance, TV, internet, magazines, food subscriptions etc. expire, try and drive down the renewal cost by speaking to and negotiating with your existing provider or leave for a new provider. To keep on top of your renewal dates and put yourself in the best position for securing a competitive renewal price, revisit your financial audit completed at Step 0 of the Framework which should capture all of your subscriptions and monthly recurring expenses and use this to then create a list of expiry dates which is then your to do list to renegotiate at the appropriate time. Use the free market to your advantage, to increase your WBF and accelerate towards your financial freedom!

House hacking:

For the vast majority of us, housing costs are our greatest expense, so any opportunity to reduce such costs should be considered. Some popular tactics include:

- Renting out a room in your house to a tenant
- Buying a multiple dwelling unit, such as a house split into two flats and rent one out whilst living in the other
- Using platforms such as Airbnb or Spareroom to temporarily rent out whole or part of your property
- Renting out your car parking space, if you are not using it

These options are not viable for everyone and may even be considered unpalatable due to the often perceived invasion of privacy or the added administrative burden, but it is important to consider all avenues on your route to financial freedom. House hacking can really help to reduce your housing costs and be an effective way to enhance your WBF (but this doesn't give you permission to buy too much house in the first place!).

* * *

Be smart with your shopping:
Becoming financially free relies on the summation of lots of small behaviour changes. A key required change is one's approach to shopping, whereby just adding in a few steps before finalising purchases can help you save money on the items you were planning on buying anyway.

You should always be on the lookout for vouchers, check cashback apps, and explore discount websites such as Facebook Marketplace, Amazon Warehouse, Gumtree and Freecycle. It is amazing how many items can be found at sizeable discounts, or even for free, just by shopping around.

I have had success with Quidco, Shopmium and Checkout Smart, earning cash back on a number of things from my utility bills to oat milk; all you have to do is remember to check what offers are available before you buy something. Do remember though that it is only a genuine saving if you were planning on buying the item anyway; it is no good buying something you won't eat, drink or use just because it's on offer.

The time of day that you do your grocery shopping can also make an impact on the price you pay; for instance, I tend to find that shopping on a weekday late evening presents the most discounted products (or 'yellow labels' as they are affectionately known in our household), which amounts to savings of hundreds of pounds over time. Like with the cash back apps, only buy things which you would buy anyway!

Key takeaways:
- The speed at which you achieve financial freedom is dependent on maximising your WBF in any way

possible by increasing your income and reducing your expenses, and then contributing the maximum amount of your WBF possible towards wealth building activity.
- You can increase your income in the following ways:
  - Ask for a pay rise
  - Work overtime wherever possible
  - Take advantage of the 'gig economy' to earn some additional income
  - Build a secondary source of income by starting your own business
- Any extra money is a good thing, but income which does not rely on your time to earn it is the best. As such, you should try and focus your time on building passive income streams.
- In addition to enhancing your WBF through increasing your income, you should also be reducing your expenses by:
  - Evaluating every expense before spending your money
  - Cooking for yourself and embracing batch cooking (saving time as well as money!)
  - Planning your meals and using a shopping list
  - Utilising technology to work from a cheaper location whilst earning money in a higher paying location – so called 'Geographical Arbitrage'
  - Realising that you are rarely rewarded for loyalty to your service providers and negotiating to get a cheaper price
  - Reducing your housing costs through 'House Hacking'
  - Shopping smart by using discount vouchers,

cash back apps, and altering the times at which you shop - small savings add up over time

Side hustles

As you are aware by now, the greater your WBF, the more money you can contribute towards wealth building activity and the faster you can achieve your financial freedom. As you will always have a baseline cost of living, there is only so much you can save through reducing your expenses and, as mentioned earlier, you should therefore focus your spare time on trying to increase your income as its potential is infinite.

A 'side hustle' is essentially a job that you do in your spare time, i.e. in addition to your main employment, and is a great way of utilising your existing skill set to increase your income and also potentially build a business profitable enough for you to leave your employment. Although the term seems to be quite a recent invention, 'side hustles' have been around for years; a key weapon in one's income-increasing armoury.

Technology has made it easier than ever to start a business. The plethora of global, online market places to sell through, the ability to build professional websites through third party platforms without the need for coding skills, and the rise of video conferencing and remote working mean you can build and run a business from anywhere at any time.

* * *

Side hustles can take various forms, it could be cutting hair, writing a blog, podcasting, buying and selling up-cycled items online, bookkeeping, washing cars, gardening, building websites for others, painting and decorating and so on. Ultimately, your side hustle could be anything, as long as you have the skills to do it. For example, this book and the financial mentoring services I offer via my website alexfennmoneymentor.co.uk are my current side hustles.

If you think this could be an income-generating route for you, here are some hints and tips based on my own experiences:

- Your side hustle should be in an area you are passionate about, as it will consume a lot of your spare time and require a number of sacrifices along the way
- Ideally it should be scalable, especially if you want it to provide a meaningful income, and not be tied to your time (as time is finite)
- It should be something you can charge for and for which there is demand
- Get the buy-in of your spouse; the sacrifices mentioned above will impact both of you so it is important to have them on board
- Consider opening a separate business bank account (there are lots of online banks that provide them) to easily identify your business income and expenses; you will need these figures for your annual tax return
- Keep a spreadsheet of your monthly business income and expenses, in as much detail as possible; it will not only help you identify where your money is going but help you understand what products/services are profitable and inform decisions about your business

* * *

In terms of business structure and practicalities, you should consider consulting an expert to review your circumstances and suggest the best structure before embarking on your side hustle. Generally speaking, it is most likely that you will follow one of two routes for your side hustle (if you are UK based and going it alone): sole trader; or limited company. If you are seriously considering a side hustle you can also check the relative costs and benefits of the different structures for yourself[1] before deciding on the best option for you. In the meantime, I have set out some of the headlines below.

Sole Trader:
This is the simplest form of business and is where the business and you are one and the same legal person, they can be set up without the need to register anything with Companies House and there is no requirement to submit your annual financial accounts to HMRC. Common examples of sole traders are self-employed window cleaners, hairdressers, decorators, etc. and all you need in order to set up as a sole trader is the knowledge relevant to your trade, required tools and paying customers!

Sole traders are taxed at the marginal income tax rate as though they are employees and need to submit a 'Self-Assessment Tax Return'. The tax payable is based on business profits, that is the income earned from the business less any appropriate business expenses such as utility bills, transport, materials, advertising and internet. The relevant income tax rate is then applied to these business profit.

Also, as of the 2021/2022 tax year, there is a £1,000 'trading' allowance whereby any income under £1,000 earned from self-employment is tax free, so if your side hustle is in its infancy and you are earning less than £1,000, you owe no tax.

As you and the business are the same legal person, you are responsible for any losses the business makes, i.e. you will have to use your personal money to pay off any liabilities the business can't meet. Equally, on the flip side, you get to keep all of the profits (after tax).

The sole trader model is arguably the best option in a side hustle's infancy, as you avoid the governance burden and associated costs faced by limited companies.

Private limited company (Ltd):
Side hustles may also be set up as private limited companies. This structure is likely best if your side hustle is growing into a full time business or is earning you a significant income.

As alluded to above, the key difference to a sole trader is that Limited companies are subjected to more rigorous governance requirements. Each year, private limited companies must produce and submit to HMRC financial statements accompanied by various other documents. It is prudent for such companies to enlist the help of a Chartered Accountant to do this which can be costly, so it is a good idea to determine how much the ongoing governance will cost you before going down this route.

Some of the main benefits of a limited company are that they pay 'Corporation' instead of 'Income' tax (which often results in a lower tax bill), and shareholders are not personally liable for liabilities as it is the company (not the individual) that enters into agreements (which offers a certain level of protection for entrepreneurs).

Summary:

Side hustles are a great way of earning additional income and developing new skills which are extremely valuable in the workplace and could even help you increase your main source of income.

I am a huge fan of side hustles due to their financial and self-development benefits and would encourage everyone to find their niche and give it a try.

hosting a dinner party at your house for at least half the cost have the same effect? Happiness is not generally found in the things you buy, it is usually felt from the company of the people around you, your experiences and having the time and freedom to enjoy them. You will find that the short term sacrifices you make to achieve your financial freedom will quickly be deemed worthwhile, especially when you no longer have to worry about money and can do what you want with your time. The time will come when your friends and colleagues around you who decided against pursuing their financial freedom journey are still complaining about trading their time in the rat race to fund their latest expenses, whilst you are packing your suitcase for your three months of stress free world travel. All of a sudden, the short term sacrifices that sounded hard or were perceived as dull and boring don't really seem like sacrifices at all; after all, they have enabled you to buy life's ultimate prize - your freedom.

I've heard leasing a car is much better value than owning a car:

This is quite a common question from my clients and one that deserves fleshing out. Firstly, I need to confess that I absolutely love cars; I subscribed to *What Car?* magazine for many years from the age of 12 and knew the stats of every new model out there. My heart still skips a beat when I see a Ferrari cruising past and, whilst I go to classic car events whenever I can, the Northern accountant in me means I am not as enthusiastic when it comes to buying them. It pains me to say it, but cars are one of the worst investments you can make, being worth only 40% of their original value at only three years'[1] old! I can't imagine you agreeing to put £10,000 of your hard earned money into an investment which will return £4,000 in three years! Even if you deposited your £10,000 into a basic savings account at 1% you would have

£10,303, three years later.

I fully appreciate that cars can be a very visible status symbol and you can spend tens of thousands of pounds on buying a new car just to show to people that you have the income necessary to afford a new car. All I have to say about this is that you shouldn't hamstring yourself financially just to prove or disprove what other people think!

You may be of the view that buying a car with cash is a thing of the past and that the contemporary 'right' way to invest in a car is to lease it or buy it through a personal contract plan, meaning you can buy your status symbol without the significant cash outlay. The average monthly car payment in the UK is just under £200,[2] or £2,400 per year. Assuming you change your car every three years, that's £7,200, and let's not forget, that's just to 'rent' the car, you won't actually own it unless you pay a sizeable balloon payment at the end of the term. Cars last a long time if you care for them properly. My view is that you should consider buying a car assuming you will keep it for at least 10 years. Because cars depreciate so quickly, a car that is 5 years old and has been well looked after would be an excellent choice, as it means buying towards the bottom of its valuation, saving yourself a lot of cash whilst still being mechanically reliable.

Still unsure? Let's assume that rather than taking out a lease car at £200 per month, you save this money instead. In just over 2 years you would have £4,800, which is more than enough to buy a good second hand car that is 5 years old. Once you have paid for the car, you can put that £200 per month towards wealth building activity and you own your car until it no longer moves! Assume your car lasts you 10 years. If you didn't own a car, and continued to lease for that

10 year period, you would have spent £24,000 on car payments and have nothing much to show for it vs your £4,800 outlay to buy a car and additional £19,200 contribution towards your wealth building activity. I fully appreciate that people need cars, but, in my opinion, it is a poor decision to direct your money indefinitely towards car payments at the expense of using your money to build wealth.

As cars don't make great investments, buy a car that is sensible, look after it and it will look after you. You might miss out on some approving glances at the traffic lights from drivers well and truly stuck in the rat race, but it is a small price to pay. Obviously this advice doesn't apply if you have more than eight zeros at the end of your bank balance and can therefore swallow £50,000 of depreciation.

Given interest rates are so low, shouldn't I invest instead of overpaying my mortgage?

This is understandably another common question I get asked by clients, given the recent low interest rates on mortgages. In theory, if you can earn a better rate of return from investing than the interest rate you pay on your mortgage, then you should direct as much of your money as possible towards your investments rather than overpaying your relatively 'cheap' mortgage debt. My counter-argument to this is that you should consider contributing a meaningful percentage of your WBF to mortgage overpayments *because* interest rates are historically low. The graph below shows the history of the Bank of England's base interest rate; since 2008, interest rates have been well below their historic average, having been as high as 17% and from the early 90s until the financial crash in 2008 they hovered around the 5% mark.

* * *

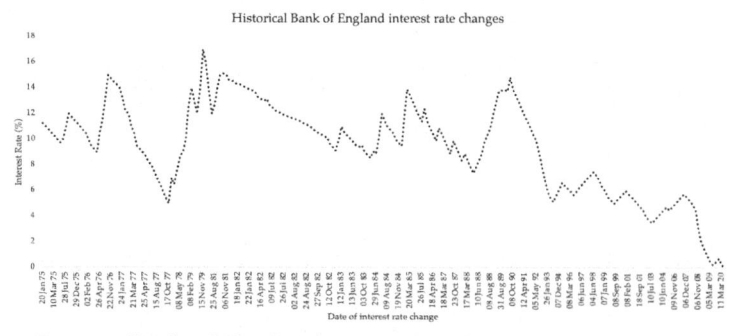

Historical Bank of England interest rate changes

Source: Bank of England

Just because interest rates have been low for so long doesn't mean they will stay that way. The UK government's response to both the 2008 financial crisis and COVID-19 pandemic was to plough billions of pounds into the economy, which will eventually lead to rising inflation and, ultimately, higher interest rates, to help curb it. This false sense of security that low interest rates will be maintained is another reason to take advantage of them whilst they are here – there may never be a better time to make significant inroads into reducing your mortgage.

As we have discussed, a mortgage is commonly someone's largest monthly expense and the single expense keeping them in their job. If suddenly they didn't have to find £750 per month to pay for their house each month, I doubt many people would be so loyal to their employer. Having minimal monthly expenses means you are nimble, it gives you options, means you can take more risks, means the pressure of the rat race reduces (or disappears) and you have the foundation of your financial fortress. Furthermore, the psychological impact of not having a mortgage or to continue the daily grind for another 10, 15 or 20 years is immeasurable.

* * *

Of course, there are no guarantees in life and health is one of the unknowns; you don't know if you will still be out walking daily at 75 or be wheelchair bound from 50. The longer you leave it to repay your mortgage, the more risk you have of not enjoying your life to the fullest extent possible. Deciding to prioritise investing whilst not overpaying your mortgage means you will have to commit to working for the remaining mortgage term. This is fine if you love your job and it hopefully means that as soon as you have repaid your mortgage, your investment account will be a lovely size enabling you to retire in a blaze of glory. There are, of course, no right or wrong answers with regards to whether you invest, overpay your mortgage or do a combination of both, as everyone's situation and preferences are unique. I have never met anyone who has regretted paying off their mortgage early, saving tens of thousands of pounds in interest payments and getting years of their life back in the process. I have, though, met countless people who are fed up in their job and dream for that big break to allow them to finally quit the rat race. I know which camp I would prefer to be in!

Personally, I adopt a hybrid approach of investing whilst overpaying my mortgage, the reason being because I intend to be in a position to be able to leave the rat race and live off my investment income as soon as my mortgage is cleared. In addition, because I am in the financial markets, I am learning the art of investing and building my confidence and knowledge which will only benefit me long-term. More importantly for me, earning my freedom from the rat race will allow me to focus full time on my business interests, taking more risks than I would otherwise be able to if I had the commitment to pay a mortgage each month. Achieving freedom and becoming the master of my own destiny is the most important thing for me personally.

You say debt is bad but I can get 0% interest on my purchases:

There are a variety of compelling interest free credit offers available in the market, from credit cards offering 0% interest to 'buy now pay later' payment options offered by major retailers such as Amazon, Klarna and Paypal to name just a few. On the face of it, this may seem like a no brainer and you may be tempted to sign up to these offers immediately but, remember, debt is debt and there is a reason these multi-billion dollar companies are offering this facility. Put simply, it makes consumers buy more, and makes the companies more money! A £600 wireless speaker system doesn't sound so expensive if you only have to pay £100 per month for the next six months.

I speak here from my professional experience; every offer, discount and promotion is worked on by a team of multi-disciplined, highly paid professionals to make sure that the company won't lose money on these types of offers. There is no such thing as a free lunch in business and this extends to these promotions; companies offer them because it ultimately means you buy more and become more embedded in their ecosystem. The rule you should abide by is to only buy things with cash; if you can't afford it, you can't have it. Only by using cash will you feel the psychological pain of letting go of your hard earned money and make the correct purchasing decision for you. This may seem like old fashioned advice, but it is advice that remains relevant no doubt hundreds of years after it was first given.

Debt, interest free or not, results in you sacrificing your wealth building fund to pay someone else for an item. Debt *is* bad and should be avoided, it's as simple as that!

I don't want to retire, I enjoy my job!

Much of the rhetoric of this book has been to save enough into your investment account to sustain you without the need to exchange your time for money with an employer. But having enough money to be self-sufficient doesn't mean you need to quit your job if it is rewarding and enjoyable; in fact, for many people, working gives them a purpose in life. Contrary to popular belief, early retirement doesn't mean you should just spend the rest of your days sat doing nothing and living an unfulfilling existence. What early retirement does mean is that you have options to do what you want, when you want, be that continuing to work full time in your current job if it brings you joy and fulfilment, working part time, perhaps starting your own business or freelancing, or alternatively working during winter and travelling during the summer; the beauty is, it is up to you!

Does working towards financial freedom mean I can't go on holiday any more?

The journey to financial freedom is a personal one, not just in terms of lifestyle upon early retirement but in terms of your lifestyle during your journey there. Theoretically, yes, there is an 'optimal' route to achieve financial freedom which involves scrimping and saving as much as possible, living on a shoestring and maximising income until you reach your number. Just because there is an optimal route though, doesn't mean you need to follow it. If you want to go on three holidays a year, have the latest phone and wardrobe, you can, but be mindful that this means pushing back the date of your financial freedom (perhaps even indefinitely). Spending money on non-wealth building activity simply means you won't be earning a return on that money and building wealth, thereby deferring your financial freedom date and trading your time for money for longer.

The same rules apply to going on holiday as to other purchases; you should save the money in a bank account separate to your emergency fund and eventually pay in cash - remember the principle, if you can't pay cash, you shouldn't spend the money!

Should I invest in a Buy to Let property instead of in the financial markets?

Investing in Buy to Let (BTL) property is often viewed as a safe, no risk investment for people in the UK and I believe this stems from the fact the British are obsessed with property ownership. Yes, you can build serious wealth through property but we need to take a balanced, informed, view before concluding that it is the silver bullet it is often made out to be.

There are many advantages to investing in a buy to let property, including the following:

- You can borrow money to fund a purchase (also known as 'leverage'), which means that you only need a 25%-30% deposit to buy a property
- There is potential to generate a monthly income from tenants, which can more then cover your mortgage payments and bills
- There is potential to generate a capital gain through the natural rise in prices or from forced appreciation (renovating the property to increase its value) or both
- Although the rental income is taxable, you can claim some expenses against such taxable income to reduce your tax bill

- There is an opportunity to purchase a house using a limited company which could reduce the amount of tax you need to pay, although running a company comes with its own responsibilities
- You can hire an agency to manage your property to take care of the maintenance and tenant queries which would make the investment truly passive, but be aware that this comes at a cost and will reduce your overall return.

There are also several drawbacks to be aware of:
- You need to pay tax on your earnings, either income tax at your marginal rate if bought as an individual or corporation tax if bought through a company
- The tax rules are increasingly going against the BTL investor, such as no longer being able to deduct mortgage interest from your tax return and instead being replaced by a flat mortgage interest rate of 20% which can significantly increase a tax bill
- If you don't have tenants, or the tenants don't pay, you still have to pay the mortgage, council tax, utility bills etc. which can cause personal cash flow pressure
- It is an illiquid asset; it can take months to sell your property, compared to if you had equities which you can sell instantly in the liquid financial markets if needed
- It is not a passive investment if you decide to manage the property yourself i.e. you can't just sit there whilst the money rolls in, you need to find tenants, manage the maintenance, submit a tax return and be the on call person in an emergency, so if the fridge breaks - expect a call, if a pipe bursts - you are going to have to resolve it
- House prices may not rise as fast as you hope/expect

and thus dent your overall return
- There are additional stamp duty land tax implications for owning BTL property which could mean you pay more tax when investing in BTL or purchasing your main family home

The return on investment with BTL can be high but the effort required and lack of tax benefits when compared to traditional financial market investments needs to be carefully considered before diving head first into BTL. There are alternative ways of gaining exposure to the property market without physically purchasing a property, for example, Real Estate Investment Trusts (REITs) which specialise in residential property can be purchased; these own hundreds, sometimes thousands of apartments and houses which they rent out and maintain, providing the return to you in the form of dividends (although you won't be able to take out a mortgage to buy them).

It is important to carefully evaluate the benefits and drawbacks of direct BTL property investment before deciding on where to invest your hard earned money. I personally have had exposure to residential property through BTL as well as REITs. In my current circumstances, I prefer to invest in a broad selection of REITs rather than BTL, as they generate a solid, passive return and I don't have to manage tenants or maintenance.

Me and my partner have different attitudes to money, what should I do?

Achieving financial freedom involves short term sacrifices, it means spending less money at a time when you are earning more, not buying as many luxuries, forgoing the latest tech and gadgets, among many other things, all of which can cause conflict in a relationship. It is important to work as a team in order to achieve financial freedom. You may be faced with the phrases 'life's too short…' and 'you still need to have fun…', in which case I would suggest sitting down and explaining the massive benefits of being able to do what you want, when you want versus the relatively small, short-term sacrifices required to get there. If you are comfortable with numbers, to help support your argument, you can even draw out the various scenarios and include the monetary values of the monthly amount sacrificed and what this means for the future. Using data and scenarios can be very powerful to support your arguments and I would strongly suggest you use prudent assumptions so as to make the financial freedom timelines achievable and realistic. The aim is to get you and your partner to understand that happiness is not found in material things but in freedom and time. When you can prove out that sacrificing a few hundred pounds per month can reclaim years of your life back, the argument is extremely compelling.

I have a poor credit score, how do I improve it?

Your credit score influences not just the amount of money you can borrow in the form of credit cards, loans, mobile phone contracts and mortgages but it also impacts the interest rate you are charged on these borrowings. The higher your credit score, the better your access to borrowing and the cheaper it is.

Your score is derived from how well you have managed money in the past and it is something that can be changed for the better (or worse). There are several ways to improve your credit score, some of which are fairly quick, others can take a bit longer:
- Sign up to a credit score agency such as Experian or

Clear Score which will help you understand your score and track your progress over time
- Register on the electoral roll at your current address
- Make your repayments on time to demonstrate to lenders that they can rely on you to repay any loans
- Keep credit utilisation low, for instance, if your credit limit is £5,000 and you borrow £1,000, your utilisation is 20%. The lower your utilisation the better as it shows lenders you are able to sensibly manage your borrowings
- Review your credit report regularly and correct any incorrect information such as previous addresses on old accounts
- Minimise the number of credit applications you make to reduce the number of searches on your credit report as it can make you look desperate for credit
- Use a specific credit builder credit card which are only issued to people with low credit scores and repay on time (to avoid high interest charges)
- Do not withdraw cash using your credit cards

There is now a plethora of information and tools available online to give you insights into your credit score and help you improve it and you should take the opportunity to do so.

Summary:

There are several talking points when it comes to financial freedom and there is no one right or wrong answer. If you want some help determining the right answer based on your specific circumstances, please do get in touch.[3]

Concluding thoughts

This chapter marks the end of the book and the start of your exciting journey towards financial freedom. You now have the knowledge and tools necessary to make achieving your version of financial freedom as easy as possible, from the fundamentals of budgeting and performing a financial audit, to investing for passive income and repaying debts, you should now feel confident to take control of your finances and create for yourself the financial future you deserve.

In the absence of formal education on personal finance, I have attempted to outline in this book that there is not just one way to look at money. I have tried to encourage you to shift your mindset away from believing you have to work for money; rather, you can make your money work for you by building multiple streams of income and achieve the ultimate goal of having control of your time and living the life you want (be that working part time, retiring abroad, starting a business, volunteering, or continuing with your current job safe in the knowledge that you and your loved ones are financially safe).

Becoming financially free will likely mean seemingly radical changes to your lifestyle but, before long, the purchases you used to look forward to making simply become an opportunity cost resulting in an increase to your 'prison sentence' of working for your employer. My advice? Embrace the initial discomfort, embrace the change to your mindset, embrace the compounding impact on your money - momentum is hard to gain, so once you have it, don't let it stop!

As we have explored, and as emphasised by the Framework, the importance of ongoing personal and professional development throughout your journey should not be underestimated; continual learning will not only help to increase your earning power but will also make the journey more enjoyable. Financial freedom is a long journey requiring discipline and sacrifices along the way, but it is vital to remember that your personal happiness should not be one of those sacrifices. Happiness is much more important than achieving an investment portfolio of a certain size by a certain age and there is no shame in deferring your financial freedom date if you are going to have a happier and more fulfilling life; whatever your destination, it is important to enjoy the ride!

I genuinely hope that this book has ignited a fire in your belly to learn more about finance and embark on your journey towards, and ultimately achieve, financial freedom. The saying *'the best time to start was yesterday, the next best is today'* has never been more appropriate and I wish you the very best of luck; not that you'll need it, after all, it really is easy when you know how.

Financial Freedom (It's Easy When You Know How)

Appendix: Applying the Financial Freedom Framework

Applying the Framework, some worked examples

This appendix compiles a couple of simple but realistic examples to highlight how the Framework applies in practice. The purpose is to demonstrate the application of the Framework, not to design a year by year detailed financial plan, so please bear this in mind when reading through.

The following assumptions have been made for both examples, to simplify the calculations and make the scenarios easier to follow:
1. Income tax rates as of tax year 2021/22
2. Inflation is excluded from pay rises and expenses
3. Investment portfolio returns are 7% per annum, adjusted downwards by 2% for inflation, giving a real return of 5%
4. Employer pension returns assumed to be 6%, adjusted downwards by 2% for inflation, giving a real return of 4%
5. Mortgage interest rate remains constant

Example 1 - Paige
Paige is 21 years old, in a graduate job with a salary of £35,000, pays 3% into her employer pension which is matched by her employer (the maximum match on offer is 5%) and is

eligible for a discretionary annual bonus. Paige has a student loan of £30,000 (plan 2) and outstanding credit card debt of £2,000 which has been balance transferred to a 0% interest credit card expiring in 18 months when the APR increases to 20%. Paige has £500 of savings in an easy access cash savings account and wants to achieve financial freedom at age 45 with an investment portfolio worth £450,000 used to generate an income of £18,000. Her journey through the Framework is outlined below.

Step 0 - audit your finances

After analysing six months' worth of bank and credit card statements, Paige calculated her monthly income, expenses and baseline WBF as follows:

* * *

Gross Income	£	2,917
Less:		
Pension deduction	£	88
tax	£	356
NI	£	254
Student loan	£	57
Take home pay	**£**	**2,162**
Expenses:		
Rent	£	750
Utilities	£	200
Groceries/food	£	250
Transport	£	150
Entertainment	£	200
Credit Card debt payment	£	100
Phone	£	50
Broadband	£	35
TV subscriptions	£	55
Clothing	£	125
Total Expenses	**£**	**1,915**
Starting WBF	**£**	**247**

The starting WBF of £247 is calculated as Paige's £2,162 take home pay less total expenses of £1,915.

Net financial position

Considering Paige's assets and liabilities, her net worth is negative £31,500. Paige is in a 'net liability' position, which is not unusual at this age given she has just left University.

* * *

Assets:

Cash savings	£	500
Pension	£	-
Total Assets	**£**	**500**

Liabilities:

Student loans (plan 2)	£	30,000
Credit Card	£	2,000
Total Liabilities	**£**	**32,000**
Net Asset / (Liability) position	**£**	**(31,500)**

Having evaluated her expenses in the context of how much value they add to her life, Paige decides to make the following monthly changes to increase her WBF:

Proposed Changes:

Cancel unused TV subscriptions	£	23
Reduce number of takeaways	£	50
Change phone contract to SIM only	£	30
Commit to buying fewer clothes	£	50
Additional WBF generated	**£**	**153**
Revised starting WBF (£247 + £153)	**£**	**400**

Following her changes, Paige's monthly WBF is now £400.

Step 1 - save one month's expenses in an emergency fund

Given the positive changes made by Paige to her living expenses in Step 0, her revised monthly expenses are now £1,762 (the £1,915 baseline less the £153 of changes). As Paige already has £500 saved in her emergency fund, she needs to save an additional £1,262 and she does this by directing her full £400 WBF to her easy access savings account for four months, outlined below:

Current emergency fund	£	500
Target one month emergency fund	£	1,762
Gap	£	1,262
WBF	£	400
Number of monthly contributions		4
New Emergency fund	£	2,100

Step 2 – maximise your employer pension contributions

Paige currently contributes, and her employer matches, 3% of her gross salary to her employer pension. As the maximum match available is 5%, as soon as her emergency fund reaches one month's worth of expenses, Paige instead contributes, and her employer matches, 5% of her gross salary to her employer pension. The impact to Paige's financial situation is as follows:

	Current Position	After Step 2
Annual Salary	£ 35,000	£ 35,000
Monthly gross income	£ 2,917	£ 2,917
Paige's pension contribution	3%	5%
Employer's pension contribution	3%	5%
Total monthly pension payment	£ 175	£ 292

Once Paige maximises her employer pension, her total

monthly pension contributions will increase from £175 to £292, an increase of £117. As a result of Paige's increased pension contributions, there is a £47 reduction to Paige's monthly take home pay as detailed in the following table:

	£	
Gross income	£	2,917
Less:		
Pension deduction	£	146
Tax	£	345
NI	£	254
Student Loan	£	57
Take home pay	**£**	**2,115**
Previous take home pay	£	2,162
vs previous takehome pay	-£	47

Paige's WBF is therefore also reduced by £47, or £50 for simplicity, so let's say her new WBF is £350 following Step 2.

Step 3 - pay off consumer debt

Paige carries consumer, debt in the form of a credit card and a student loan. As clearing her student loan is not a priority, Paige's focus will be on clearing the credit card debt that is remaining four months into her financial freedom journey. This is done by contributing her full WBF towards her credit card repayments in addition to her already recurring monthly payment of £100, as outlined below:

* * *

WBF	£	350
Debt at start of financial freedom journey	£	2,000
No. of repayments since starting financial freedom journey		4
Monthly debt repayments	£	100
Debt balance to clear	£	**1,600**
Add WBF to current debt repayments	£	**450**
Number of months in which debts are cleared		4

After a further four months (eight months into Paige's financial freedom journey), Paige's credit card debt is completely cleared. At this point, Paige's monthly expenses are reduced by £100 and her WBF increases by an additional £100 to £450 per month.

Step 4 - increase your emergency fund

It is at this stage that Paige can comfortably increase her emergency fund to cover three to six months' worth of expenses (between c.£5,000 and c.£10,000). As Paige is stable in her job and has no financial dependants, she decides to build up her emergency fund to £7,500, achievable within 12 months (as outlined below):

* * *

New monthly expenses	£	1,662
Current emergency fund	£	2,100
3 month emergency fund value	£	4,986
6 month emergency fund value	£	9,972
Target emergency fund	£	7,500
WBF directed to emergency fund	£	450
number of months to contribute		12

By the end of this stage, Paige, who has been following the Framework for 20 months has a fully funded emergency fund, is maximising her employer pension and has no consumer debt, a solid foundation to start investing for financial freedom.

Step 5 - attack your mortgage

As Paige does not have a mortgage, this step can be skipped.

Step 6 - invest, invest, invest

In order for Paige to generate the desired level of £18,000 in passive income per annum, Paige would need an investment portfolio worth £450,000 by her target financial freedom age of 45. Paige achieves this as follows.

Between ages 24 and 30, Paige begins investing her monthly £450 WBF and an annual bonus of £1,250 into her investment portfolio which, assuming a 5% growth rate, will be worth just over £45,000 in six years.

* * *

Starting portfolio value	£	-
Monthly contributions (WBF)	£	450
Annual WBF contributions	£	**5,400**
Annual bonus	£	**1,250**
Age now		24
Age @ end		30
Annual return (excl inflation)		5%
No. of years of contributions		6
Portfolio value after 6 years	£	**45,233**
Annual income (4% withdrawal)	£	1,809

During this time and as part of Paige's ongoing development, she studies for a professional qualification in her spare time to increase her prospects at work. Upon completion when Paige is 30 years old, she receives a promotion, and her salary increases from £35,000 to £45,000 (which equates to an extra £412 per month in take home pay) and is eligible for larger annual bonuses. Also from age 30 and in addition to her new job, Paige, an avid amateur crafter starts to sell homemade crafts online, generating an additional monthly income of £275. Paige's new WBF is therefore £1,137 (baseline WBF of £450 plus £412 from the new job plus £275 from crafting).

Paige directs this new WBF of £1,137 and annual bonuses of £3,000 to her investment portfolio for fifteen years which results in a portfolio worth just over £450,000 and can provide Paige with just over £18,000 income per year should she draw down 4% of her portfolio annually.

* * *

Portfolio value at age 30 (from above)		£45,233
Monthly contributions (new WBF)	£	1,137
Annual WBF contributions	**£**	**13,640**
Annual bonus	£	3,000
age now		30
age at financial freedom		45
no. years contributing to the portfolio		15
annual return (excl. inflation)		5%
Future value of portfolio	**£**	**453,101**
Annual income (drawing down at 4%)	£	18,124

While Paige has been building her investment portfolio, she has continued to contribute to her employer pension scheme in line with Step 2 of the Framework. Assuming Paige stops these contributions at age 45, her employer pension pot will be valued at just over £222,000 by the time she is age 57, £329,000 at age 67 and £450,000 at age 75, which provides *additional* income of approx. £9,000, £13,000 and £18,000 respectively. This puts Paige in the position to do whatever she likes, in the comfort that, even if she never invests another penny into her investment portfolio or pension, she will have enough passive income to support her desired lifestyle from age 45 (with the added benefit of an income boost from her employer pension from age 57). Paige has achieved her financial freedom and hasn't thought twice about those surplus TV subscriptions she cancelled at age 21(!).

Example 2 - Tom

Tom is 30 years old working full time and earning £42,000 per year and is eligible for a discretionary annual bonus. He contributes 4% of his salary to his employer pension which his employer matches (the total match available is 6%). Tom lives in a house worth £250,000 with a mortgage of £200,000, has a student loan (plan 1) with £30,000 outstanding, credit card debt of £4,000 on a 0% interest rate which expires in 21 months' time, an emergency fund of £1,500 and a fully paid for car worth £5,000.

Tom's financial freedom goal is to have a fully paid for house and an investment portfolio generating £10,000 in passive annual income by age 50.

Step 0 - audit your finances

After analysing six months of bank and credit card statements, Tom calculated his monthly income, expenses and baseline WBF as follows:

* * *

Gross Income	£	3,500
Less:		
Pension deduction	£	140
Tax	£	463
NI	£	324
Student loan	£	165
Take home pay	**£**	**2,408**
Expenses:		
Mortgage	£	1,036
Council tax / utilities	£	180
Groceries/food	£	200
Fuel	£	150
Entertainment	£	150
Credit Card debt payment	£	225
Car Insurance	£	50
Home Insurance	£	30
Savings	£	-
Phone	£	90
Broadband	£	40
TV subscriptions	£	30
Clothing	£	125
Total Expenses	**£**	**2,306**
Starting WBF	**£**	**102**

Tom's starting Wealth Building Fund of £102 is his take home pay (£2,408) less his expenses (£2,306).

Net financial position

Considering Tom's assets and liabilities, Tom's net worth is £62,000:

* * *

Assets :

Cash savings	£	1,500
Pension	£	40,000
House	£	250,000
Fully paid for car	£	5,000
Total Assets	**£**	**296,500**

Liabilities:

Student loans (plan 1)	£	30,000
Credit Card	£	4,000
Mortgage outstanding	£	200,000
Total Liabilities	**£**	**234,000**

Net Asset / (Liability) position	**£**	**62,500**

Having evaluated his expenses in the context of how much value they add to his life, Tom decides to make the following monthly changes to increase his WBF from £102 to £377, or £375 for simplicity:

Reduce clothes shopping	£	100
Eat out less	£	80
Change phone contract to SIM only	£	70
Eliminate short car journeys	£	25
Additional WBF generated	**£**	**275**
Revised starting WBF (£102 + £275)	**£**	**377**
WBF used for simplicity	**£**	**375**

Step 1 - save one month's expenses in an emergency fund

Given the positive changes made by Tom to his living expenses, Tom revisited his financial audit at Step 0 resulting in a revised figure for expenses of £2,031 per month (£2,306 baseline, less the £275 of expense reductions). As Tom already has £1,500 saved in his emergency fund, he needs to save an additional £531, and he does this by directing his full £375 WBF to his instant access savings account for two months until his emergency fund reaches £2,250, more than enough to cover him for one month's expenses.

Current emergency fund	£	1,500
Target one month emergency fund	£	2,031
Gap	**£**	**531**
Monthly WBF contributions	£	375
Number of monthly contributions		2
New Emergency fund	**£**	**2,250**

Step 2 - maximise your employer pension contributions

Tom currently contributes, and his employer matches, 4% of his gross salary to his employer pension. As the maximum match available is 6%, once his emergency fund reaches one month's worth of expenses, Tom increases his pension contribution to, and his employer matches, 6% to take advantage of the full match. The impact on his financial position is as follows:

	Current Position	After Step 2
Monthly gross income	£ 3,500	£ 3,500
John's contribution	4%	6%
Employer's contribution	4%	6%
Total monthly pension contribution	**£ 280**	**£ 420**

* * *

Once Tom maximises his employer pension, his total (individual plus employer) monthly pension contributions will increase from £280 to £420, an increase of £140. As a result of Tom's increased pension contributions, there is a £56 reduction to Tom's monthly take home pay as detailed in the following table:

Gross income	£	3,500
Less:		
Pension deduction	£	210
Tax	£	449
NI	£	324
Student Loan	£	165
Take home pay	**£**	**2,352**
Previous take home pay	£	2,408
vs old takehome pay	-£	56
New WBF after pension max	**£**	**319**
WBF used for simplicity	**£**	**320**

Tom's WBF reduces from £375 to £319 (or £320 for simplicity) as a result of increasing his pension contributions.

Step 3 - pay off consumer debt

At the start of his financial freedom journey, Tom had a credit card balance which he transferred to a 0% interest credit card. During the two months it took him to build up his emergency fund, Tom continued to pay £225 towards the credit card debt and now his outstanding loan debt is £3,550. As Tom's student loan debt attracts less interest than the return his money can earn by paying off his mortgage and investing, he decides not to prioritise paying off his student loan, instead only focusing on paying off his credit card debt in this step.

Tom directs his revised WBF towards his credit card repayments in addition to his already recurring monthly payment of £225 until it is fully cleared, which takes around seven months. It is also important to remember that, from this point, Tom does not spend any more money on credit, his expenses are covered using cash.

	£	
New WBF		**320**
Debt at start of financial freedom journey	£	4,000
No. of repayments since starting financial freedom journey		2
Monthly debt repayments	£	225
Debt balance to clear	**£**	**3,550**
Add £320 WBF to current debt payments (£225)	£	545
No. of months debts cleared in		7
Also reduces monthly expenses by	£	225

Once his debts are cleared, Tom's monthly expenses reduce by the amount equal to his repayments (£225) and therefore his WBF increases to £545.

Step 4 - increase your emergency fund

Tom now turns his attention to increasing his emergency fund to cover three to six months' worth of expenses. Due to the reduction in his monthly expenses, it will take less time to build up his emergency fund. Tom has decided to save around £7,000, which takes him nine months to do.

* * *

Revised monthly expenses	£	1,806
Current emergency fund	£	2,250
3 month emergency fund value	£	5,417
6 month emergency fund value	£	10,835
Target emergency fund	**£**	**7,000**
WBF directed to emergency fund	£	545
number of months to contribute		9
Emergency Fund after 9 months	£	7,155

By the end of this stage, Tom, who has been following the Framework for 18 months, has rightsized his monthly expenses, cleared his consumer debts, has an emergency fund to cover up to four months' worth of expenses and is maximising his employer pension contributions.

Step 5 - attack your mortgage

As identified at Step 0, Tom has a mortgage on his house which, following 18 months of mortgage payments, is just under £191,000. Having evaluated various combinations of overpaying his mortgage and investing, Tom decided to contribute £150 of his £545 WBF each month to overpaying his mortgage (and £395 to his investment portfolio).

These overpayments will result in Tom completely clearing his mortgage in just over 17 years, when he is around 49 years old. This is in line with his financial freedom goal. An additional benefit is that, at this point, his monthly expenses reduce by the cost of the mortgage repayments (£1,036) and his emergency fund automatically covers an additional 5 months of expenses.

Once Tom's mortgage is paid off, his WBF increases from £545 to £1,581.

Step 6 - invest, invest, invest

Alongside clearing his mortgage, Tom chose to invest the remaining £395 of his £545 WBF into his investment portfolio (comprising of 90% global equities, 10% global bonds). Tom has also been investing his annual bonus of £4,000. By the time Tom has paid off his mortgage at age 49, his investment portfolio is worth around £236,000 which will provide an annual income of £9,430.

Current portfolio value	£	-
Monthly contributions (WBF)	£	395
Annual value of monthly WBF contributions	£	**4,740**
Discretionary bonus	£	4,000
Age now		32
Age @ end		49
Annual return (excl inflation)		5%
No. of years of contributions		17
Est. future value of portfolio	£	**235,739**
Annual income (drawing down at 4%)	£	9,430

Following the repayment of his mortgage, Tom's WBF increases from £545 to £1,581 which he contributes for one year, from age 49 to age 50, this results in a portfolio worth just over £270,000 which can sustain an income of just under £11,000 per annum. Tom has therefore reached his financial freedom goals of having a fully paid for house and a portfolio which can provide an income of £10,000.

* * *

Potfolio value once mortgage paid off		£235,739
Monthly WBF contributions	£	1,581
Annual value of monthly WBF contributions	£	18,969
Discretionary bonus	£	4,000
no. years contributing		1
Annual return (excl inflation)		5%
Total future value	£	**270,495**
Annual income (drawing down at 4% p.a.)	£	10,820

In addition to this, Tom's employer pension will be worth just under £234,000 (assuming it returns 4% excluding inflation) when he hits his financial freedom goal at age 50. Should Tom never contribute another penny to the pension, it could be worth £346k by age 60, £512k by age 70 and £623k by age, providing *additional* annual income of approx. £14,000, £20,000 and £25,000 respectively. Tom has achieved his financial freedom objectives with a c.£7,000 emergency fund, a fully paid for house, an investment portfolio from which he can generate an annual income of c.£11,000 and a sizeable employer pension!

Summary:

These examples are designed to demonstrate how the Framework can be applied to, albeit heavily simplified, real life situations. Although everyone's financial situation is unique and there is no one size fits all approach, I hope that they provide you with useful guidance for applying the Framework yourself.

Preface

[1] https://www.yorkshirepost.co.uk/business/consumer/almost-eight-10-adults-will-be-carrying-debt-2021-3079284
[2] https://www.ons.gov.uk/peoplepopulationandcommunity/personalandhouseholdfinances/incomeandwealth/bulletins/householddebtingreatbritain/april2016tomarch2018
[3] https://www.helpguide.org/articles/stress/coping-with-financial-stress.htm#
[4] https://www.finder.com/uk/pension-statistics

Introduction

[1] https://www.theguardian.com/money/2018/jan/25/uk-workers-chronically-broke-study-economic-insecurity
[2] https://ppcprotect.com/blog/strategy/how-many-ads-do-we-see-a-day/
[3] https://uk.finance.yahoo.com/news/credit-borrowing-ten-myths-truths-you-need-know-050012047.html?guccounter=1
[4] https://au.finance.yahoo.com/news/revealed-the-20-happiest-countries-in-the-world-for-2021-210035590.html?guccounter=1&guce_referrer=aHR0cHM6Ly93d3cuZ29vZ2xlLmNvbS8&guce_referrer_sig=AQAAALGkN6Fdn8r6sgEEReAFGjrqt1vVZ58oNWyRvn8EwAMIqDkHxHeAu2hbyli-RC3FoBmM1f4xq4jKKityGIu59MQhpldPzf-Hqgiwr3RFOdzedJTEwsR-5-wrPr0i_ubrlioAWihjZKDfgw-4lvpdIP0L0SEvbPleuT7KIuHuvsqr

* * *

What is financial freedom?

[1] https://www.thegazette.co.uk/companies/content/103466
[2] https://networthify.com/calculator/earlyretirement?income=70000&initialBalance=0&expenses=23800&annualPct=5&withdrawalRate=4

All you need to know about debt

[1] https://www.which.co.uk/news/2019/09/revealed-the-cost-of-moving-house-tops-10400/
[2] https://www.gov.uk/student-finance

All about pensions

[1] https://www.which.co.uk/money/pensions-and-retirement/starting-to-plan-your-retirement/how-much-will-you-need-to-retire-atu0z9k0lw3p

A brief introduction to investing

[1] https://backtest.curvo.eu/market-index/msci-emerging-markets
[2] https://en.wikipedia.org/wiki/Bond_market
[3] https://money.cnn.com/retirement/guide/investing_bonds.moneymag/index3.htm
[4] https://www.ig.com/uk/trading-strategies/what-are-the-average-returns-of-the-ftse-100--200529
[5] https://www.forbes.com/sites/johnjennings/2020/09/23/beating-the-market-is-simple-but-not-easy/

Approaches to investing

[1] https://www.ig.com/uk/trading-strategies/what-are-the-average-returns-of-the-ftse-100--200529

Budgeting techniques

[1] https://www.moneyandmentalhealth.org/wp-content/uploads/2019/03/debt-mental-health-facts-2019.pdf

* * *

The financial freedom mindset

[1] https://millionairefoundry.com/millionaire-statistics/

Framework Step 1 - save one month's expenses in an emergency fund

[1] https://financiallyhappy.ltd/how-much-does-the-average-person-have-in-savings-uk/
[2] https://www.cnbc.com/2021/01/11/just-39percent-of-americans-could-pay-for-a-1000-emergency-expense.html

Framework Step 2 - maximise your employer pension contributions

[1] https://www.actuarialpost.co.uk/article/highest-average-pension-pot-is-less-than-90-000-9269.htm

Framework Step 3 - pay off consumer debt

[1] (https://www.nationaldebtline.org)
[2] https://www.yorkshirepost.co.uk/business/consumer/almost-eight-10-adults-will-be-carrying-debt-2021-3079284

Framework Step 4 - increase your emergency fund

[1] https://financiallyhappy.ltd/how-much-does-the-average-person-have-in-savings-uk/
[2] https://financiallyhappy.ltd/how-much-does-the-average-person-have-in-savings-uk/

Framework Step 5 - attack your mortgage

[1] https://www.nimblefins.co.uk/average-uk-household-budget

Ongoing activities for financial freedom

[1] https://www.statista.com/statistics/281936/average-salary-by-education-level-in-the-united-kingdom-uk/

* * *

Side hustles

[1] https://www.gov.uk/set-up-business

Myths and common questions

[1] https://www.theaa.com/car-buying/depreciation
[2] https://www.nerdwallet.com/uk/personal-finance/cost-of-car-ownership/
[3] alexfennmoneymentor.co.uk